D1109087

# And I His Servant

# CONTENTS

# FOREWORD

Though acclaimed a missionary statesman and a close friend of such evangelical luminaries as Navigator, founder Dawson Trotman, first Youth for Christ president Torrey Johnson, and evangelist Billy Graham, Dr. Dick Hillis wanted most to be known as "a very ordinary man living in extraordinary surroundings but faced with very ordinary problems."

In compiling this selected anthology of his refreshing and powerful writings, it became increasingly clear that this was more than a catchy phrase, but a life faithfully lived. He wrote so little about himself but very much about God's preeminence in his life, about God's incredible care and provision in the most extreme situations, about his beloved Chinese workers, and about those he considered true heroes of the faith.

In fact, in Part III of this book the reader will find about the only two chapters in his writings that give a clue as to the nature and incredible extent of his eight-year ministry in the troubled and hazardous China of the 1930s and '40s.

Dick's heartbeat for the lost is dramatically shown in Part I where he writes of putting God's will ahead of the beautiful girl he deeply loved, of Chinese peasants pathetically turning to gods of mud and straw, and of millions for whom religion was "little more than a security blanket."

In Part II you will see Dick's greater concern for serving the Lord than for his personal safety demonstrated in four incredible stories of when God "Unlocked the Heavens."

And when it came to his ministry in Taiwan and the rest of the world after being kicked out of China by the communists, you will read in Part IV, again not of his personal exploits, but of some of the talented and committed men who "climbed and conquered" as missionaries with Overseas Crusades (now OC International), the lengthening shadow cast by founder Dick Hillis.

"This is so great," Dick is quoted as saying in the epilogue written by Keith Brown. "I began my ministry in China fifty years ago, and now that I'm toward the end of my life I'm able to finish my ministry back in China." Dick was referring to the Voice of Friendship Seminary radio program broadcast by the Far East Broadcasting Company and supported by Dick and OC. Beamed to almost every nook and corner of the vast China mainland, this program continues Dick's ministry of reaching the lost and training pastors and leaders in China long after he could physically be present there, even after he went to be with the Lord!

Dick's prayer as a young missionary in China was, "Let Christ be Lord and I His servant." For the next sixty years of his life and ministry, Dick consistently took up the towel and modeled servanthood. Though Dick has now gone to receive his eternal reward, his servanthood legacy is being carried forward by the 360 missionaries of OC International as they live out Dick's vision to see the nations reached for Christ through serving national church leaders around the world.

Greg Gripentrog
President, OC International

# Part 1
# Concern For the Lost

"The command of the Lord of the harvest is
that the Gospel should be preached to every
person in every nation in every generation."

# Breaking the Sound Barrier

From *Not Made for Quitting,* Dr. Dick Hillis (Minneapolis, MN: Dimension Books, 1973), chapter 20, "Breaking the Sound Barrier"

I was "called" before I was "saved." Yes, our terms — "called," "saved," consecrated," "committed" — are seldom big enough to fit our experiences. And our God is so much bigger than our terms that He can turn them around to suit His own purposes.

The first inclination God wanted me in China came when I was thirteen years old and a freshman in high school.

Our little Methodist church in the great Northwest set aside one week each year for evangelistic meetings. My folks attended every meeting. To please them, Don, my twin brother, Harry, our older brother, and I went along. Going got us out of tiring homework and gave us an opportunity to see "the gang."

In 1926, Dr. George Bennard, the author of "The Old Rugged Cross," was invited as the evangelist. I confess I have no idea of the content of any of Dr. Bennard's messages, least of all what he said on that Thursday evening. He did not speak on missions but when he gave an invitation to accept Christ, I came under such conviction that God wanted me to be a missionary to China that I rushed to the wooden altar rail to tell God I would go.

Long minutes later I stood up and left the altar. As I walked out to the Model A Ford, I was aware that China was my destination and God was my Boss.

In the car on the way home I told Mother and Dad of my decision to be a missionary. Their reaction was one of real joy. "We gave you to God before you were born," Mother said. For a few months I really worked at this new enterprise. But the tide was too strong. Other things were just more interesting – school, the gang, football, and the excitement of staying free to run my own life. As the months passed I discovered that it takes more than a trip to the altar to make a missionary. Becoming a missionary seemed unreal and far away. I tried…I failed…so why not forget the whole thing.

I soon eased back into the main current of high school life. Now and then I experienced a twinge of conscience. I had made a vow to God and gone back on it. But so, I told myself, had millions of other people.

Strangely, I found it easier to cloud God from my thoughts than to wipe China from the horizon. The great cosmopolitan city of Shanghai intrigued me. Its multiracial populace promised more opportunity and excitement than any city in the world.

I dreamed: When high school days were over I would leave home, cross the Pacific, and drop out of sight amidst Shanghai's colorful multitudes. Ten years later I would re-appear, a bright star out of the East, to dazzle my parents with the fame and fortune I gained in Cathay.

Wild dream? Of course! But God condescendingly mixed a large portion of His plan with a little of my plot. Before my story ends you will see how I went to China with *Him* rather than alone.

My part was to become restless and go to California. Although I loved my parents, I rebelled against a little town, little church, and little people. I would go to a big city like Los Angeles and be big with it.

God's part was to get me from Los Angeles to Shanghai. Now between Los Angeles and Shanghai there is a lot of water, and between my dream and God's design were two hundred and eight weeks and twice that many miracles.

The first big miracle took place on Sunday evening in the Church of the Open Door in Los Angeles. My twin brother had entered Biola to prepare for the ministry. To be with him I also entered Biola, so we were both in church that night.

At the altar the Holy Spirit brought to my heart the peace that only comes with the assurance of salvation. Now I grew excited about discovering God's will for my life. I determined to find it…and to obey. God's first gracious move was to teach me something about a walk of reliance upon Him.

"Faith without works is dead," and work I did. To me each job came as an answer to prayer. On the day I was about to go without eating, a restaurant called for a bus boy. Or a lady gave me work waxing her kitchen floor or pruning her fruit trees. I proved God faithful.

The teaching at Biola was not simply academic. Men of God presented the Scripture in such a way that it took on flesh and blood. I felt that I must be a missionary *now*, not at some future date. There were plenty of opportunities, and I took many of them: Sunday school classes…street meetings…jail services…rescue missions…Gospel teams…and preaching assignments.

I could not take in the rich truths of the Gospel without giving them out. I would bust. I was getting more than lessons and theology. I was meeting a *Person* face to face and *meeting Him* impels one to introduce Him to others.

And what happened to the China dream? I was too busy to think about China. After all, I was a missionary of sorts in Los Angeles.

Honesty forces me to admit that the sight of a lovely girl also played a part in making a foreign land less attractive. I first saw her at a Biola banquet.

"Did you notice that attractive, smiling brunette sitting across from you, Ken?" I asked.

"Notice her? You guess I did, Dick. Couldn't take my eyes off her."

After a little spy work Ken reported, "Her name is Margaret Humphrey. She is eighteen, a serious Christian, and a good student. And as of this moment she is not with anyone."

Whether she had a boy friend in her home town of Yakima, Ken did not know.

I had gone with girls. Some I liked. Some I didn't. From that night on I could not get Margaret off my mind. I watched her in class. I used any excuse to get close enough to talk with her. As I sat in my squeaky study chair, her pretty face would flash before me and I would dream.

I managed one date – tennis together – before she started going with a friend. Now my lonely avenue became prayer. I wrote her name on the top of my prayer list and asked God to give her to me. She became my one concern. She was more important than China or the man across the street...more important than anything.

As the class moved through the first three chapters of Romans, the Holy Spirit so illuminated the truths that it was like coming out of the long night of an Alaskan winter. First, the awfulness of millions being lost without Christ set up such a mental conflict that for a time I questioned that "God is love."

But as I struggle and studied, the Holy Spirit took me to the Hill of the Skull. There I realized that the love and holiness, the wrath and justice of God are simply part of His perfect immutable character. Does Calvary speak of unsurpassed love or of righteous wrath? Both! Righteous wrath toward sin and abiding love toward the sinner. "He that spared not his own Son" (Romans 8:32, KJV) forever satisfied me that God loves lost mankind. Now I heard the cry of the millions across the sea. They suddenly became my personal responsibility. I could not avoid, and do not think I really wanted to, those searching questions Paul asks in the Book of Romans:

"But how shall they ask Him to save them unless they believe in Him? And how can they believe in Him if they have never heard about Him? And how can they hear about Him unless someone tells them? And how will anyone go and tell them unless someone sends him?" (Romans 10:14-15, *Living Letters*).

But was it China or was that simply a boyhood dream? I set about to find out. Each week I went to the library to study the people and customs of a different country.

I bought a National Geographic World Map and in alphabetic order prayed for different countries each day.

At the sacrifice of other things I made it a point to hear every missionary speaker possible.

Every missionary biography I could get my hands on I read.

I sought out missionaries to question them about their work and the needs on their fields.

In order to understand "faith missions" I asked three to put me on their mailing lists.

The more I searched the more intense grew the conviction that God did want me to serve Him in China. But this seemed so insane. God knew, better than I, that language was by far my poorest subject. Even with a sympathetic teacher and some special tutoring, the best grade I could pull in Spanish was a "D." And my conscience told me I hardly deserved it. It just did not make sense. It was so illogical that I should go to China to a people whose language is one of the most difficult in the world.

Another thing did not make sense. The Chinese language is tonal and I am only one grade point above tone deaf. One should be musical to speak Chinese and artistic to write its characters. I am neither musical nor artistic and, to add insult to injury, I possess a good forgetter.

How could I be expected to retain thousands of Chinese characters – characters that to the novice look like they were written by a drunken chicken?

"No," I said to myself a hundred times, "it just isn't logical. God does not want me in China. What if I went, flunked the language, and came home a missionary casualty? Such action certainly would not bring glory to God."

As I struggled with this problem, I was reading through the Book of Exodus. Assuring God and attempting to reassure myself that if it were not for the "language problem" I would gladly go, I opened the Word of God. It was Wednesday and my reading was in the fourth chapter. In verse ten I was struck with the excuses Moses made for not obeying Jehovah's orders:

"I am not eloquent," he complained.

"I am slow of speech, and of a slow tongue."

My excuses were not too different from the ones Moses made in his encounter with God. I felt rebuked.

"And the Lord said unto him, Who hath made man's mouth? Have not I the Lord?" (Exodus 4:11, KJV).

In the same way God answered Moses' arguments some three thousand years ago, He now talked to me, "Dick, who made your mouth? Have not I the Lord?"

Thoughts raced through my mind with such rapidity they tumbled over one another. In obedience situations that seem illogical become reasonable. Does not acceptance of God's will guarantee success? Will He not enable me to do whatever He appoints me to do? Does not the treasure in an "earthen vessel" bring more glory to the treasure? Is it not like God to give you the task and even send you to the place that is hardest for you so that His grace can be more fully manifest through you?

Like a man whose cataracts were removed so he could see again I saw that God had a right to send me any place and that I had a right to believe He would see me through. God stops Moses' arguments with a command to obey and a promise to enable. "Now therefore go, and I will be with thy mouth, and teach thee what thou shalt say" (Exodus 4:12, KJV).

That morning God gave me the same command and assured me with the same promise. My response was not sensational but it was sincere, "I will go, Lord, and trust You to teach my mouth the Chinese language."

Beside the verse I wrote, "God's *promise* to me for China." *God kept His promise* and after a few months of struggle with strange Chinese words, I broke the sound barrier.

And what about that girl? Here also God was faithful. Seven years after I first laid my eyes on her lovely face, we stood together in the city of Hankow, China, and repeated our sacred marriage vows.

God never withholds what is best for you if you are in His will. Why should He? And why should you delay in discovering His will?

When you pray, "May Your will be done here on earth, just as it is in heaven" (Matthew 6:10, *Living Gospels*), you are asking God to work out His will in your life on earth as perfectly as the angels in heaven perform His will.

Have you been mumbling words or do you mean it? The fruit of *"my will"* is frustration and failure. The fruit of *"Thy will"* is life – exciting, fulfilling, and meaningful.

And what must one do? Sincerely and honestly pray, "May Your will be done," and then put muscles to your words. And what do I mean by muscles?

The men and women in this book [see chapters 11-13–eds.] believed God wanted them in foreign service. Their belief determined their actions.

Did they face problems? Plenty of them.

Were they ever perplexed? You know they were.

Did discouragement threaten them? They are human.

Were obstacles thrown in their paths? Mountains of them.

These common heroes were led to climb. Though sometimes faced by winds of adversity and storms of protest, they overcame problems and, in the Name of the One Who told them to climb, conquered. They learned that to climb one must add

> to vision, determination;
> to determination, preparation;
> to preparation, perseverance;
> to perseverance, patience;
> to patience, plodding.

They discovered that decision is five percent and follow-through is ninety-five percent. Their stories have been told to encourage you to climb. Your problems are not too different from the ones they faced.

They climbed and conquered.

You, too, were born to climb!

# In His Footsteps

As you grow older, you look back on your life and thank the Lord for those who had a deep and profound influence on you. Dick Hillis was one of those men in my life. His passion to see men and women come to the Savior was contagious and his example of commitment, discipline, and vision inspired me.

Anna Belle and I joined OC because of his leadership, as we wanted to be part of an organization which attracted outstanding men and women who responded to his vision.

In many ways I followed in his footsteps: we both graduated from Biola, both went to Asia as missionaries, both came back to head up the Missions Department at Biola, and both led OC.

From the first time we met when I was a student, to the last time we communicated when I sang to him in Chinese and he joined in even though he had not spoken a word for months, his warmth, love, and influence will be with me always. Anna Belle and I thank the Lord for the blessing of knowing Dick and serving with him.

Clyde Cook
President, Biola University

# Sincerely Yours

From *Is There Really Only One Way?*, Dr. Dick Hillis (Santa Ana, CA: Vision House Publishers, 1974), chapter 1, "Sincerely Yours"

I have watched thousands of worshipers in the Orient bow before man-made gods. My first reaction was to silently ridicule. How stupid and naïve can they be? I thought.

They hire a carpenter to nail the wooden "bones" together and a mason then fashions the muscles and flesh with wet mud. For a little higher price or bigger meal, he will form a female deity. When the mud is dry, a local artist adds brilliant colors to the drab mud god. Then under the watchful eye and practical guidance of a golden-robed priest, the idol, after being given an altar and incense burner, is dedicated as the all-sufficient village god.

But before I made a further judgment about their sanity, I decided to ask why they bowed before these idols. "Madam," I said, "for the last ten minutes you have been on your knees bowing before that deity. Would you please tell me why?"

"Sir," she replied, "My husband is out of work. My children are hungry. The landlord has threatened to throw us out. My burdens are heavy and I am asking for help."

"And you, Sir," I said, "I noticed you gave a bushel of rice to the priest. Then as the temple bells began to ring the priest shook a box filled with bamboo sticks until one fell on the ground. Would you please tell me what all this means?"

"The bushel of rice," said the man, "is my offering to our god. The bamboo stick has an answer to prayer inscribed on it."

"And what was the priest praying for?" I asked.

"We have seven children. The youngest is two weeks old. Her mother is very sick. The midwife can't stop her bleeding. She has a fever and won't eat and I am afraid for my children and their mother's life."

The answer to why people bow before gods who have eyes and cannot see and ears and cannot hear, is simple. They have burdens they cannot carry and fears they cannot quiet. They have never met the One who said, "Come to Me, all who are weary and heavy laden, and I will give you rest" (Matthew 11:28ff).

Another question crossed my mind as I stood in the temple compound. Are these idol worshipers sincere in their beliefs? But then the question backfired as I thought about my own sincerity and the sincerity of the average Christian who attends an average morning church service. Are these more sincere than those who prostrate themselves before a mud god?

When I want a "study in sincerity" I watch worshipers in a heathen temple. Their faces are laced with worry and concern; one sees no nonsense or laughter and I am forced to conclude if sincerity could save, many of these people would be saved. The hard fact is that sincerity does not, cannot, save! It's possible to be absolutely sincere and at the same time, absolutely wrong.

One of the most sincere men in the New Testament was a Pharisee named Nicodemus. Most of the Pharisees, however, were anything but sincere. And Jesus reserved His harshest words of condemnation for the Pharisees' counterfeit piety calling them "whited sepulchres". But Nicodemus was of a different stripe. He carefully fulfilled every ritual of the strictest religious Jewish sect. He was a religious man and no one questioned his deep sincerity. Yet with all his faithful religious practices he knew something was missing. His faithful religious practices did not quiet his guilty conscience, give him peace with God, or take away the fear of dying and standing before a holy God. Nicodemus was sincere but lost, and he sensed it. If sincerity were enough, this ultra-religious Pharisee would never have turned to Jesus.

Today, a man like Nicodemus would be considered an ideal member of many churches – even a candidate for deacon or elder. After all, wasn't he a highly respected member of the Sanhedrin, brilliantly educated, law-abiding, and ethical in his conduct? He held high moral standards and, as we have noted, his religious sincerity was beyond question. But like the thief on the cross, he was lost because there is no salvation in sincerity.

Sincerity is of no value if you put your trust in your sincerity. On the other hand, if in honest sincerity one admits that his religious sincerity does not save and turns to the Savior, as Nicodemus did, such sincerity is to be praised. Nicodemus was so sincere about making his peace with God that when Jesus hit him with the profound statement, "Truly, truly, I say to you, unless one is born again, he cannot see the kingdom of God" (John 3:3), he didn't question the necessity of the new birth. His question wasn't "why" but "how" (John 3:4).

That night Nicodemus dropped his dependence upon his sincerity and good works, and the man who for many years had been "sincere but lost," was saved through faith in the One he secretly interviewed. "Whoever believes that Jesus is the Christ is born of God; and whoever loves the Father loves the *child* born of Him" (1 John 5:1). What human sincerity cannot do the divine Son of God can.

As Nicodemus was sincere, but lost, equally so, the idol worshiper is lost, no matter how sincere he may be. And he can only be saved as Nicodemus was saved – through a personal encounter with Jesus Christ.

# My Privilege for Ninety Years

It is thoughtful of the editors of this book about my brother, Dick, to invite me to add a few thoughts about him.

Dick and I have enjoyed knowing one another for more than ninety years. We can both truthfully say, "Thank You, Lord, for giving us such a privilege." His life and ministry have brought inspiration and blessing to me and to many others. For this I thank my Lord and Savior.

We spent the first twenty years together as we went through elementary school, high school, and Bible school together. Then Dick went to China as a single young missionary not yet twenty years old. And I went to India, also still single. It was eleven years before we saw each other again. We had both married, and rejoiced as we recounted to one another the leading of the Lord in our individual lives. We could each say, "My Good Shepherd led me all the way."

Thank You, dear Lord, for giving me the privilege of living with a twin brother who has been such an inspiration to me and thousands of others.

Don Hillis
Dick's twin brother

# I Got Religion

From *Is There Really Only <u>One</u> Way?,* Dr. Dick Hillis (Santa Ana, CA: Vision
House Publishers, 1974), chapter 4, "I Got Religion"

A ll men have some form of religion. Men are, in fact, incurably religious. But does religion save? Does religion bring peace with God?

During my years in the Orient I talked with thousands of devotees of the great ethnic religions and found many to be deeply religious. But as I probed below the surface I discovered deep unrest.

"Do you work at your religion?" I asked.

"Yes."

"Do you feel your misdeeds are forgiven?"

"I cover them with my good deeds and offerings."

"Do you have fear about facing death?"

"Yes, I am afraid to die."

"Where will you go when you die?"

"I am not sure."

"Does your religion give you satisfaction of mind and joy of heart?"

"Not really, but I have nothing else."

"I have nothing else" – what tragic words! But are we to blame because they have *nothing else?* Let's answer this question by asking, "What is religion?"

Among other things, I believe religion is a ceremonial service caused by guilt and fear. It's Satan's counterfeit for salvation and a cover-up, not a blotting out of sin. It's the self-effort of man, not the saving grace of Jesus Christ. Religion leaves its devotee hoping for divine approval but never knowing; wishing but never certain.

I have been challenged for "imposing my *religion* on the people in the Orient." Invariably their objection is that America is a young upstart nation and Christianity, compared to other religions, is in its adolescence. The people of the Orient are proud of their rich religious heritage, art, poetry, and strong moral philosophy. Why destroy all this by imposing our Western religion? I have also been accused of destroying family unity and upsetting the lives of those to whom I have taken the Gospel. I have been told I was doing an injustice to people to come to them as a Christian missionary. I want you to know I wouldn't turn over in bed for religion…but I would circle the world for the sake of the Gospel!

I once asked one critic if he felt Christianity was just another religion like all the rest.

"Religions are like windows," he replied. "They may be different is size and shape but they all perform the same function. They let God's light in and they allow us to view God."

This is oversimplification. After all, man gets into heaven through a door, not a window. Jesus said, "I am the door; if anyone enters through Me, he shall be saved, and shall go in and out, and find pasture" (John 10:9).

To suggest that we not communicate the love of Christ to those who have not heard would indicate the Gospel has nothing to offer them. I believe Christianity has everything to offer religious man. From a spiritual standpoint, man has retrogressed rather than progressed in spite of his religious efforts. This clearly indicates that man's religious escalator only runs downward (Romans 1:23).

The dictionary classifies Christianity as a religion, but we must remember it's far more than that. Some schools teach a course called "Comparative Religions" and include Christianity among the many religions studied. This raises the question: Can one *compare* the Gospel with religion or do we find more truth in *contrasting* the two? My missionary friend, Dr. John T. Seamands, gives some powerful contrasts in his book, "The Supreme Task of the Church":

"Religion is man-made; the Gospel is God-given.

"Religion is what man does for God; the Gospel is what God has done for man.

"Religion is man's search for God; the Gospel is God's search for man.

"Religion is good views; the Gospel is Good News.

"Religion is good advice; the Gospel is a glorious announcement.

"Religion takes man and leaves him as he is; the Gospel takes a man as he is and makes him what he ought to be.

"Religion ends in an outer reformation; the Gospel ends in an inner transformation.

"Religion whitewashes; the Gospel washes white.

"Religion places the prime emphasis upon doing; the Gospel places the emphasis on a Person.

"You can take Buddha out of Buddhism and Buddhism still remains with its four noble truths and its eight-fold path.

"You can take Mohammed out of Islam and Islam is still intact with its five pillars of action and its six articles of belief.

"But if you take Christ out of the Gospel there is nothing left, for the Gospel is Christ."

Christianity is a *life* – the life of Christ implanted in the heart of man. Christianity is unique in that it alone has a living Author. No religion dare claim this distinction.

In the heart of China stands a large ornate Confucian temple. The main courtyard surrounds a mound of dirt over sixty feet high. Yearly, thousands burn incense before that mound. They believe the skull of Confucius is buried beneath the pyramid of dirt. It may well be, for the founders of all the great ethnic religions are dead.

I have not visited Mecca but millions of ardent Muslims have. Why? To pay their respects to the remains of Mohammed, the founder of the Muslim religion. Of man, God said, "For you are dust, and to dust you shall return" (Genesis 3:19). The dust of Mohammed remains in Mecca.

Not long ago I visited an empty tomb in Jerusalem. Is it the actual tomb in which the body of Christ was placed by Joseph and Nicodemus? One must not be dogmatic. But the Christian is positive that Christ conquered death and the grave. He arose from the grave, broke the Roman seal, shoved the great stone aside and ascended into heaven. This is the uniqueness of Christianity. Christ came to save men from sin and religion. And one of the powerful proofs of His Saviorhood is the empty tomb.

For millions of people religion is little more than a security blanket. If you doubt this take an informal poll and ask each person if they are a Christian? You will discover a variety of answers. "I get to church as often as I can." "I go to church every Christmas and Easter." "I don't swear, drink, or smoke." Others who are asked this question raise their voices and emphasize the strength of their religious conviction with, "What do you think I am, a pagan?"

Such mistaken attitudes did not begin with the *now generation*. Religion was born in a beautiful garden millenniums ago: "...And they (Adam and Eve) sewed fig leaves together and made themselves loin coverings" (Genesis 3:7). Our first parents attempted to cover their disobedience and sin by their own efforts and this is exactly what "religion" is all about. Apart from the intervention of God, man's way will always be the way of fig leaves – works and religion. Wise Solomon reminds us, "There is a way which seems right to a man, But its end is the way of death" (Proverbs 14:12).

Who better illustrates the difference between religion and salvation than Adam's first-born son, Cain? (See Genesis 4:3-5.) Cain was no different than most of us. He felt the need of doing something to please God. He possessed an inner consciousness of a holy God. He experienced deep guilt because of conduct he knew was wrong in the sight of God. As a religious man he searched for a way to quiet his constant awareness of guilt. Cain was religious.

The Bible says, "So it came about in the course of time that Cain brought an offering to the Lord of the fruit of the ground" (Genesis 4:3). Cain possessed real convictions about a man's duty toward a holy God and came up with the idea of appeasing God with an offering from his fields.

Today the vast majority of mankind follows Cain's example. The heart of their religion is offerings of fruit, rice, incense, and good works.

One does not question the sincerity of Cain. Remember, he did not murder his brother until after his self-devised religion had failed. Nor does one question the sincerity of many who are involved in the thousands of sects, cults, isms, and religious creeds of today. If sincerity alone could save, there is little question that many religious people would be saved. But sincerity alone is not enough. Just as one can be sincere and sincerely right, so one can be sincere and sincerely *wrong.*

Adam's first-born, Cain, was sincerely wrong even if we grant him the quality of sincerity. Cain was no agnostic. He believed in

God. And it would seem he believed in salvation, even if it was a fig leaf, an "I-must-save-myself" salvation – a salvation of works. And that is the cornerstone of all religion.

It would be incongruous for Adam not to teach his sons that God, not man, is the Author of true salvation. Had he not told his sons that God ripped off the fig leaves of personal effort? Certainly he reported to Cain and Abel that the skins they now wore were provided by God through the death of an innocent substitute. How would younger brother Abel know this without older brother Cain's knowledge? Cain's problem was that he was religious, proud, self-sufficient, and unbelieving about God's way of salvation.

In many ways Cain's offering was more attractive than Abel's. Who wants to stare at a lifeless bleeding lamb? Isn't golden grain more appealing? Yes, let's admit some religions have areas of remarkable beauty. But beauty does not save. God saw in Abel's lamb the figure of the coming "Lamb of God" who would take away the sin of the world. In Cain's offering of grain God saw the beginning of man's efforts to save himself.

Is it possible to follow religious rites and be lost? A thousand times, yes! Religion (man's works) has never opened the door of heaven to a single soul. All men without the Lamb of God are lost.

Religion is Satan's counterfeit for God's salvation. Christianity is God's answer to Satan's religions.

# You Guys Are All Chicken!

Dick had the gift of challenging young men! It was at a summer camp in 1938 that I first heard the name Dick Hillis. He was just back from a term in China as a missionary. I didn't know him from Adam, but his messages burned deep into this high school kid's memory. (In that era the majority of missionaries were women.) At the evening campfire the flickering flames helped to enhance Dick's heart of passion as he shouted, "Where are the men? You guys are all chicken!"

Dick came to the States in 1953 to incorporate his fledgling organization and to recruit a team. He also wanted to meet and share notes with my brother and his wife, who had been under house arrest together with the Hillis family in Shanghai.

As an afterthought my brother invited Betty and me to have lunch with this guy Hillis. My brother said, "Remember the man at Mount Hermon who shouted, 'You guys are chicken!' He'll be here!" This would be a divine appointment.

Dick's awesome challenge stirred our hearts as he described the Filipinos' love for basketball and the opportunity for the Gospel. Then he said, "Chuck, the Philippines needs coaches like you. A hundred men would gladly take your place (coaching) at Wheaton College, but it would be difficult to find even one man to go to the Philippines. Besides, your war experiences can be an open door to the hearts of the Filipinos."

Dick was right, and we were on our way to fifty years of fruitful service!

Chuck Holsinger
OC missionary to Asia

# Who Killed "Concern"?

From *Is There Really Only Ơne Way?*, Dr. Dick Hillis (Santa Ana, CA: Vision House Publishers, 1974), chapter 10, "Who Killed 'Concern'?"

To have a "clean heart" is healthy but to reach the lost, one must have a "concerned heart."

Have you ever wondered what happened to the word *concern?* It may not be considered an old-fashioned word, but it's an old-fashioned idea. Most of us today are too busy to be concerned with anyone but ourselves. We have little or no time to care about the lost and, subconsciously, have put God on our "charity list." This is contrary to our Lord's attitude and those who followed Him. Scripture is filled with evidence of Christ's concern for others:

When Lazarus died, Jesus was *concerned* and gave the dead man life.

When the sinful woman was condemned He was *concerned* and forgave her.

When the temple was dirty He was *concerned* and cleansed it.

When the Pharisees judged and accused He was *concerned* and warned them.

When the unclean lepers cried for healing He was *concerned* and cured them.

When the thief was dying beside Him on the cross He was *concerned* and took him to heaven with Him.

Christ spelled CONCERN with capital letters. The Apostle Paul was so *concerned* for his people that he was willing to take their place in hell if by doing so, Isaac's children could have his place in heaven (see Romans 9:1-3).

Paul's' *concern* for the Gentiles was just as deep. The anguish of his cry, "Woe is me if I do not preach the gospel" (1 Corinthians 9:16), reveals the strong pulse of this *concern.*

The first century Church was *concerned* about the lost in Samaria and the hungry in Jerusalem. The Church prayed and sent out anointed witnesses across Asia and Europe. Like her Lord she spelled CONCERN with large letters.

The nineteenth century Church was also *concerned* and sent men across every ocean in search of lost multitudes. Hear them:

"Give me Scotland or I die."

"I feel as if I cannot go on living if I cannot reach the millions in the vast inland provinces of China."

These are the heart sounds of men who spelled CONCERN with capital letters. By contrast, this word is seldom heard and too infrequently practiced today. The starving, sick, enslaved, suffering, lost, and dying are everywhere. Their number increases by thirty-four million every year. Is anyone deeply *concerned?* There is little evidence. What happened to the word?

Who put this beautiful word to death? Was she poisoned with the soft drink of selfishness, strangled by the clutching grasp of materialism, smothered by a heavy blanket of indifference? In what coffin did they lay her? Is there hope of her revival?

In answering these questions I condemn myself. Because, I, like you, had a part in her death. We were her pallbearers. But the casket is not yet closed and there is hope of resuscitation. We must pray for "the love of Christ" which flows silently and smoothly like liquid mercury to fill our empty hearts with compassion and *concern*. We desperately need a working compassion that spells *CONCERN* with capital letters.

"If a brother or a sister is without clothing and in need of daily food, and one of you says to them, 'Go in peace, be warmed and be filled'; and yet you do not give them what is necessary for their body; what use is that? Even so faith, if it has no works, is dead, being by itself" (James 2:15-17).

We will never find this new compassion if we continue to put our own concerns ahead of God. He must come first in our lives. Our offerings to Him must no longer be "the things we can no longer use." We must give Him the "firstfruit." Most people know this, but forget. I am glad our loving Father knows we need to be prodded. Not long ago He stirred me into action with the return of the robins. The birds returned to Palo Alto on the tail of a flooding rainstorm and looked as soaked and sorry as my soggy front lawn. Deciding they needed some loving encouragement, I started toward the back door with a fresh loaf of bread. Then suddenly an "economic plot" flashed across my mental computer. With bread costing half a dollar a loaf why give them fresh bread? Wouldn't stale bread be good enough? Rummaging around I found just the thing – some pieces so stale they were a little moldy! "If the robins are hungry enough," I reasoned, "they will accept my moldy offering."

I crumbled the stale bread, scattered it on the lawn, and stepped inside to watch through a window. I felt good as I saw the robins cautiously alight on the lawn and ravenously accept my entire offering. Oh, I forgot to tell you, birds are on my charity list!

Feeding the robins triggered a surprising train of thought. I had just offered God's feathered creatures something I couldn't use and didn't want. Was I guilty, consciously or unconsciously, of giving the Creator of those feathered fliers the same kind of offering? The more I pondered the idea the more troubled I became.

As a missionary, I have seen a lot of "moldy bread" given to God. Some of the correspondence in my letter file reeks with mildew. A man once wrote, *"We are getting a new car. We can't get anything for our old one. Could the mission use it? Would it be possible to give me a tax deductible receipt for the blue book price?"*

Was that a "moldy bread" offering? It certainly wasn't "fresh bread." Was the writer's heart motivated by love for God and concern for His creatures or was God simply on his charity list?

Another letter said, *"Our church is sending three boxes of clothes for your missionaries. They are not new, of course, but some of them are quite nice. I am sorry we did not have time to get them cleaned. Our ladies' missionary society is paying the postage so there will be no cost to the mission."* That is *concern* of a kind, but what kind?

In both cases there seemed to be a parallel between the bird offering of "bread I couldn't use." Let me hasten to say we are grateful for every loving gift. What I am talking about are *attitudes* in giving – attitudes of true concern.

And then there was that telephone call. The voice was warm and congenial. *"We are buying a new grand piano,"* she said. *"We have an old upright. It is nearly thirty years old and is still in good condition since no one plays the piano around here too much. I planned to give it to the Goodwill, but my husband thought the mission might want it."*

"Yes," I told her, "the mission would appreciate such a gift."

But as I think back, I wonder if it wasn't "moldy bread" in God's sight. Did they conceive of God as waiting around for a handout?

Do you see what I mean? Have we formed the habit of giving God used objects we no longer need because we've replaced them with something better for ourselves? This certainly is not the way God treats us. Then do I have my priorities in order? What does Jesus say about priorities? "But seek first His kingdom, and his righteousness; and all these things shall be added to you" (Matthew 6:33).

As one studies this verse the word "first" takes on new meaning. God in no way forbids me to provide for my family. On the contrary, the Bible warns, "But if any one does not provide for his own, and especially for those of his household, he…is worse than an unbeliever" (1 Timothy 5:8). It is the order of priority that is important. The first fruit of my talent and toil is to be gladly given to Him. Christ and His cause are to be my "first" concern. Then He promises everything else will fall into proper order and I will lack nothing.

Come to think of it I can't remember ever receiving a letter reading: *"We were going to buy a new car (or whatever) for ourselves, but as we prayed about it the Lord told us to use the money for the extension of His kingdom. Enclosed please find a check. We want the mission to use it to get the message of life to those who are facing death without Christ in Vietnam. It is a joy to do this. We are not worried, for our Heavenly Father has promised to take care of our old car. You see we have claimed the promise, '…first His kingdom…all these things shall be added…' We cannot tell you how very concerned we are for those who are lost."*

Take special note of the "action" words in our Lord's conversation with the serious rich young man in Matthew 19:21. *"Go…sell…give…* and you *shall have* treasure in heaven." How contrary to one's practice of "hurry…purchase…keep." Here Jesus tells the young man (and us) that what one gives, he keeps, and what one keeps, he loses.

This point becomes crystal clear when I restudy the invitations Jesus gave men to follow Him. When he called Peter and his brother Andrew to "follow," they immediately left their nets, and followed Him (see Matthew 4:19-20). Later when Jesus asked the brothers, James and John, to give up their fishing business, they did so immediately (see Matthew 4:22). God's plan was more important to these four young men than their own plans and possessions. His *concerns* became their *concerns*.

Notice the difference, however, to the reply of two other young men to the Lord's invitation. "Permit *me first* to go and bury my father," said one. And the second said, "I will follow You, Lord; but *first* permit *me* to say good-bye to those at home" (Luke 9:59, 61). In each case the youth put his personal concern "first." When he finished doing this thing then he would have time to be concerned about God's thing.

Is it not contradictory to call Jesus "Lord," then tell Him we will give Him what He wants only after we have done what we want? Isn't it rather like putting Him on our charity list and saying, "When I have a spare moment I will pray," or, "If I have a spare dollar at the end of this month I will see that you get it?"

Recently a young man told me his goal was to make a million dollars before he was thirty. *He assured me when he reached his goal he hoped to serve God with his time and money.* Was he feeding robins with "moldy bread"? Did he have his priorities right? The answer is no. His first concern was for himself after which he hoped to find time for God

There was nothing I could do to change this young man, but with thought and honest obedience *I* can change and take God off my charity list and begin seeking *first* His kingdom. I can come to my Father and admit my own self-seeking. I can ask Him to change my attitude. I can stop long enough to ask Him to fill my heart with His *concern* for lost men and women.

# Part II
# The Heavens Unlocked

"He had unlocked the heavens, giving us
milk and men...just when we needed thcm."

# Curtain of Darkness

From *Unlock the Heavens,* Dick Hillis (Henderson, NE: Service Press),
chapter 1, "Curtain of Darkness"

E arly on the morning of December 6, 1934, Chinese
Communist troops stormed the walls of Tsingteh. This
ancient town of South Anhwei Province had once been
known as the "City of the Kings." John and Betty Stam, ambassadors
of the King of kings, were now living there. Before the Stams could
flee, the Reds thundered at their door.

After being held captive for 24 hours, they were taken 12 miles
across the mountains to the town of Miaosheo. John wrote to the
leaders of the China Inland Mission:

DEAR BRETHREN:

My wife, baby and I are today in the hands of the
Communists. All of our possessions...are in their
hands, but we praise God for peace in our hearts.
God grant you wisdom in what you do and us
fortitude, courage, and peace of heart. He is able and
a wonderful Friend in such a time. The Lord bless and

guide you. As for us, may God be glorified, whether by life or by death.

In Him,

John

That night Betty was allowed to lie down, but John was tightly bound to a post of the bed. Early the next morning they were led through the streets of the city, painfully bound by ropes and stripped of their outer clothing. As they marched to their deaths, the Communists cried to the people to come and watch the foreign devils die.

On a little hill outside the town, John was ordered to kneel. A flash of the sword brought quick release. Bound as she was, Betty fell on her knees beside her loved one. Those who witnessed the tragedy testified to the calmness with which John and Betty faced the worst their misguided enemies could do.

On that cold December day I was in the neighboring province of Honan. I was just twenty-one, and had been in China one year and one month. The martyrdom of John and Betty Stam came as a rude shock. Lurking, insidious questions now came out into the open. Should I retreat? This was more that I had bargained for. Satan's darts were different from anything I had faced at home. Was it worth it all? Was I, like John and Betty Stam, throwing my life away?

In the "rat race" that is America I had often longed to be alone – to be quiet and get away from people. Now the experience I once craved was my defeat. I discovered that loneliness is not just a lack of people. After all, I was surrounded by people – the people whom I had come to serve. For them I had left home and loved ones. I knew I was not really alone; I still had God's promise, "Lo, I am with you always" (Matthew 28:20).

But loneliness can't always be rationally dismissed. The mud walls of my home shut me in. I tried to sing, and the dull echo of my voice mocked me. Defeat seemed inevitable.

My discouragement was heightened by my trouble with the Chinese language. Each character looked to me like the scratches of a drunken chicken. As I was almost tone deaf, the different tones meant nothing to me and my attempts to speak the language confused my listeners. Satan's suggestion became almost attractive to me as he whispered, "You'll never get this mixed-up language. What's the use? You're wasting your life and you know it. Why not head for America?"

It wasn't that I had expected an easy time when I began my missionary service in China. I knew I was being drafted into God's army and was moving toward front-line duty. I thought I was prepared to fight and to die, if need be. Now, however, I was prepared to surrender. I had come to the end of the road. God may have cared for His servant, Elijah, but I felt He had forsaken me.

One day, out in the province of Honan, I found myself on my knees. I was not there to pray. I was ready to go home and was searching for an excuse to do so with the least possible disgrace. I knew it was impossible for me to remain on the field. I could not preach victory and live in defeat. But to return home had its problems. I thought of the money people had invested in sending me to China. When asked why I had left the field of battle, what answer would I give? Should I stay and be a hypocrite…or go home in apparent failure? What was the answer?

At the same time, in a modest home in Pasadena, California, it was midnight. A little woman had been sleeping peacefully for three hours, but suddenly she was wide awake, as though an unseen hand had shaken her. As she lay there, she became aware that someone was in need of prayer. She tried to brush aside the conviction that she ought to get up and pray.

"After all," she thought, "I have been faithful in my prayer time each morning."

The urge to pray increased. She obeyed the prompting of the Holy Spirit and, switching on the light, knelt down by her bedside. As she prayed through her prayer list, she came to the name of a young man who had been in China less than two years. She had never met him, but she had seen his picture in a missionary magazine and had faithfully prayed for him each day. Now she felt a strong burden for him. Was he in some physical danger? Or was he facing some spiritual conflict? She did not know. But in the intensity of her burden all she could do was cry, "Dear God, see him through...see him through."

As I knelt in a mud hut in faraway China, the battle raged in my discouraged heart. After nearly two hours of agony, a strange quietness settled upon my restless soul. In the stillness, the One who had promised to go with me and never leave me nor forsake me gave me a very simple but straight message: "Don't doubt Me. I will see you through...I will see you through."

In the darkness of midnight a woman in Pasadena prayed. At that very hour in faroff China God took away the darkness and spiritual disaster that overwhelmed a defeated soldier. God unlocked the heavens, and defeat was turned into victory.

# DIRTY TRUCKS TO WASH

In the fall of 1950, Uri Chandler, Dick Hillis, and I were the first OC team to go to Formosa. We bunked together in an upstairs bedroom in the home of Jim and Lil Dickson, Presbyterian missionaries. Our daily schedule was filled with meetings as we rushed around the island in an old Dodge panel truck that someone had donated. It rained a lot, and the roads were muddy, and the truck looked awful. One afternoon, Hillis said, "Culver, I want you to go down and wash the truck." I was the 24-year-old "junior" team member and frankly, I didn't particularly want to go wash the truck; besides, I had some paperwork to do. So I got busy at my desk – a few minutes passed and I looked out the window and down in the yard below was Dick, bucket and water in hand, scrubbing down the dirty truck.

Dick never said a word, and I have never forgotten that lesson in servant leadership. Needless to say, there were many "dirty trucks to wash" over the years, but I never forgot the first one. Dick Hillis was a great mentor…a true servant of God.

Ells Culver (1927-2005)
Co-founder/Senior Vice President
Mercy Corps, Inc.

# Angel Escort

From *Unlock the Heavens*, Dick Hillis, (Henderson, NE: Service Press),
chapter 3, "Angel Escort"

In the darkness of midnight an angel guided the Apostle Peter through the gates of jail into the freedom of the streets. I have had a similar experience, although I must admit that the angel escorts God chose to guide me had rather soiled wings.

In 1941, my wife Margaret, our two young children and I lived in the city of Shenkiu in the great teeming province of Honan in Central China. One night sharp pains in my abdomen roused me out of a deep sleep. I immediately suspected appendicitis, and when my groans awakened Margaret, I told her of my fears. There was no sleep for the rest of the night, but there was much praying. At daybreak we decided that I should hire a rickshaw and head off for the nearest mission hospital.

The journey was not easy. Due to the war that was raging at the time between the Japanese and the Chinese, all roads had been torn up, plowed, and some of them actually planted with wheat. My rickshaw pullers made very slow progress and, in spite of my thick fur-lined gown, the freezing temperature added to my misery. When we were within three hours of our destination, we saw Japanese planes come over and drop their bombs – hitting both the hospital and the railroad station. I knew in that town there would be no relief for my pain, although I did manage to find a doctor. He diagnosed my illness as appendicitis, but the only advice he could give me was that I should return to Shenkiu, pick up my wife and children, and start by a devious route to the big hospital in Shanghai.

As I returned to Shenkiu to gather up my little family, the Holy Spirit very graciously reminded me, "Nothing is yours." When I gave myself to Christ in 1930, I meant my dedication to be total, but now I realized that I had unconsciously taken back some of the things I had given to God. I was acting as if they were my own. Now the constant pain in my side seemed to remind me that life itself was not mine – that should the appendix burst I would be buried in a shallow grave on the Honan plain. God faithfully brought home the message, "Nothing is yours. Life, health, strength, wife, and children – all are merely loaned to you. They are to be used for God's glory. Nothing is yours."

During our last two days in Shenkiu, Margaret packed four suitcases and we took the tops off the rickshaws, so that all we had were the "ricks." Suitcases were placed at either end, and Margaret sat down between the suit cases on one of the rickshaws – taking baby Margaret Anne, aged three months, in her arms. I settled myself in another rickshaw with our seventeen-month-old son, John. Wonderful Christian pullers promised to take us as far as they could go.

Before leaving, Margaret brought before the Lord a petition for milk for her babies and for men to open up doors – doors that would take us through the Chinese front lines, through no-man's-land, through the Japanese fighting force, and on to Shanghai. She claimed the promise, "The angel of the Lord encampeth round about them that fear him" (Psalm 34:7, KJV). We would need men and miracles.

Our first day out ended in discouraging defeat, for we had gone only a short distance when we were forced to turn back because of heavily falling snow. It was a cold, bleak house that gave shelter to my family and me that night, and it was easy for our spirits to sink.

The next morning the snow had stopped falling, so once again we headed for the front lines, which we must cross in order to get to Shanghai. On the evening of the second day of travel, we arrived at the headquarters of the defending Chinese Army – on the southern bank of the San River. When I went to see the commanding officer to request permission to cross the battle lines, he thought I was crazy. He himself was in an overhappy state through too much wine. He informed me that he was expecting the Japanese to attack at any moment, and it would mean certain death to step across the lines into no-man's-land. He also told me that in the area between the two great armies groups of bandits were plundering anything and everything that had been left by the fleeing people. If we should get caught by these bandits, we would receive worse treatment from them than from the Japanese.

However, in spite of his words of caution, the tipsy officer wrote out a paper giving me permission to cross the river. I am sure in the back of his befuddled mind was the thought that when he retreated he would need my house for his headquarters. Here was a fair swap – a house for a piece of paper.

Now that we had our permission to proceed, we needed a place to spend the night. But how could we ever find a house in this little town that was already crowded with soldiers? As I left the general's headquarters, the son of a fine Christian saw me. Although this son had broken his father's heart with his wickedness and was now smuggling opium and other goods back and forth across the lines, he at once asked us if he could do anything to help.

When we told him of our plight he led us to a little mud lean-to. True, there were no doors or windows, but at least it was a shelter. We immediately put down our oilcloth, unwrapped our bedding, and by the light of a peanut-oil lamp ate our meager supper. In the marketplace I had been able to buy some steamed bread, a big bowl of steamed sweet potatoes, and some hot flour-and-water gruel. With these we satisfied our hunger and that of our little boy.

Just at daylight the next morning the smuggler led us to the edge of the river, where we found a boat he had chartered for us. We were taken across the river and several miles into no-man's-land. As the smuggler left us, returning to his river headquarters, we thanked God that we were still alive and we rejoiced in His gracious goodness in providing our smuggler "angel."

It was not easy to find our way, for there were no roads and on those dull February days the sun could not be seen. But unseen angels seemed to lead us along the right path. To encourage our hearts, the faithful rickshaw pullers broke out into a lovely Chinese hymn, taken from John 14, "Let not your heart be troubled: ye believe in God, believe also in me."

No-man's-land was desolate – miles of flat, snow-covered fields dotted with small deserted villages. The people had fled west in their retreat from the Japanese. The doors and windows of their homes gaped open – a paradise for plundering bandits.

Progress was slow – too slow for a sick man. When would we ever reach Shanghai? We were tired, discouraged, and running out of both food and milk. Did God have any more angels? Did He see our weary company? Would He unlock the heavens for us once more?

As the sun began to set on the second evening of our journey through no-man's-land, we prepared to settle down for the night in an abandoned house in a large deserted village. As I was on my knees rummaging through a suitcase, I was startled by a rough voice saying, "Chi-lai, stand up."

It didn't take a look at the guns pointing at me to make me understand that we had been captured by a group of roving bandits.

The leader, in sharp, crisp barks ordered his men to take our four suitcases, and then demanded that I turn over all my money. Reaching for my wallet, I did what comes so naturally in China – I handed him my name card and asked him his "honorable name."

The simple question angered him. Was I trying to identify him so I could report him to the general? Enraged, he cursed at me. Then a sudden change came over him as he stared at my name card.

With an expression of perplexity, the leader searched my face and exclaimed, "Why, your name is the same as mine!"

This was unusual, for in eight years in China I had never met anyone with the same name as mine. My language teacher had given me a very strange Chinese surname – one completely unused in that section of Honan. Grasping at a straw, I said to him, "Kind sir, we are brothers, members of the same family! We are now united!"

"It is true," he answered. "You are my elder brother."

Turning to his soldiers, he ordered them to return all of our goods and to see that everything was put back into place. He assured me he would do his duty, for I was his elder brother. He forgot that I was an American and he was a Chinese – that my face was white and his face was yellow. We had the same surname, and this made us brothers. He ordered his men to unroll their blankets for sleep, and that night bandits and missionaries slept together.

True to his promise, our bandit "angel" provided his best man as a guide for our continued journey across no-man's-land. In the middle of the afternoon we came within sight of the Great Walled City. Our guide left us there after informing us that just outside the city were the Japanese lines. We did not know how to proceed, but committed ourselves to God and moved forward. Suddenly, two Japanese sentries stood before us and shouted something at us which we could not understand. I took off my hat, shouted back to them in English, and cautiously walked up toward the pointed guns.

The soldiers began to search our goods carefully, jabbering at us in their unintelligible language. However, their sign language was easy to understand, for after a few minutes of haranguing, they moved behind our pullers, stuck their bayonets in their backs and ordered them to march up to the gate of the Great Walled City.

By this time the sun was setting and we were tired, sick and hungry. We had prayed on the road that we might be able to get inside the city to a little church and that we might have some privacy and an opportunity for a bath, but our chances for such luxuries seemed remote. At the gate a battle of words began between the guards and the sentry who had captured us. The guards had been ordered to let no one inside the gate. They were adamant; they were not going to open the gate for us. Did it mean God had run out of angels? Were we to have no rest, food, and sleep that night?

Suddenly we heard the sound of galloping horses, and three Japanese officers rode up. The one in the center had two stars on his shoulders – a two-star general. To my astonishment, he addressed me in perfect English. "Where in the world did you come from?" he asked.

I told him my story: I was a missionary and was sick and needed to get to a hospital. We needed rest, baths, and milk. I also politely asked him where he had learned such perfect English.

Without hesitation he informed me he had attended the University of Washington in 1936.

"General," I said, "give me the pleasure of introducing to you one of your fellow alumna. My wife was also at the University of Washington in 1936."

At this the general beamed with amazement and delight and greeted my wife warmly, promising to fulfill any requests he could. My wife asked for a quiet place to rest and told of our need of milk for the baby. The general immediately barked some orders in Japanese to his men, then turned to his fellow alumna of the Class of 1936 and promised, "You shall have all that you have requested. In the morning I will give you a pass to take you on through Japanese lines. You will find milk at the little church, for the former missionary owned a cow."

The great gates creaked open to admit us. The people of the city were amazed as they watched our tired, dirty little party proceed to the Christian church. Perhaps no one was more surprised to see us than the lovely old Bible woman, who threw her arms around my wife and chattered in sweet, friendly, Christian conversation. The cow was milked, water was heated for our baths, and we spent a restful night in the little mud and straw church. The next morning the general provided a pass and an escort to take us safely outside the city.

As we approached the next big city we wondered how the Japanese there would receive us. There was a small church in the suburb, but would the Japanese allow us to remain there or would they take us on into the city? We reached the outskirts of the suburb just after dark. For the last half hour John had been quite excited, talking to me in his baby fashion. I now told him to keep quiet. I do not know how much he understood but he kept quiet. As we approached the suburb guards, they challenged, "Who are you and where are you going?"

I answered in Chinese, "We are Christians. We are going to the little church right here in the suburb."

The darkness hid our identity, and the guards did not trouble to spot us with their flashlight. Fortunately, they were satisfied with my Chinese language and never imagined that I was a foreigner. The password was given to me.

We were welcomed warmly at the little church. Much to our surprise, we discovered that a foreign missionary was still living there. He had sent his family home as the Japanese moved toward his city, but had determined to stay himself. Walking into his inviting living room – with its warm fire, electric lights, and cozy comfort – we heard, for the first time in eight years, the music of "The Old Fashioned Revival

Hour" broadcast. Our gracious host, God's loving angel, set about preparing beds, baths, and food, and that night we slept as we had not slept for many a night.

The next morning our new missionary friend escorted us to the train station. Here we said a sad farewell to six angels who had used the muscles of their bodies to pull us across many a dangerous mile. After a long and hazardous train journey, we arrived at Shanghai. Soon I was in the hospital, had my operation, and began my recovery.

Now you have heard my story. Is it any wonder that the words, "The angel of the Lord encampeth round about them that fear him," are more than mere words to me? As the army of angel escorts parades before my mind's eye, I thank God for every one of them – a Chinese general with a little too much under his belt, a wayward smuggler, an unpredictable bandit, and a Japanese general – all put to service by my Lord that they might take care of His little children. I do not know where they are now. Nor will I ever know. But my heart still rejoices in God's love and faithfulness. He had unlocked the heavens, giving us milk and men in strange ways and strange places, but always just when we needed them.

It is a fact, not a cliché, that "He careth for you" (1 Peter 5:7, KJV).

# JUST KIDS OUT OF COLLEGE

How immeasurably thankful we are to Dick Hillis, who saw our potential for mission work when we were just kids out of college. We were eager to serve but very immature.

But Dick believed in us. He taught us largely by example. We lived next door to the Hillis family in Taiwan for six years. He set an example for us in every area. He was a godly man, lived a Christ-centered life, and worked with the confidence that God was leading and directing. His was a contagious spirit that encouraged and challenged us all. It was consistent over time and permeated every facet of his life.

He gave us job assignments that were well beyond our natural abilities and expected us to accomplish them with a minimum of supervision. When we blew it he was faithful to correct us. At the same time he lavished praise when a job was well done. He also knew how to have fun and be our friend.

He suffered the dangers of war while raising six children, lost his wife, Margaret, to cancer, was often afflicted physically, and still maintained a positive, God-focused outlook on life. We watched and learned how to live and how to work.

His love for Christ knew no limits. He brought many to Christ and stamped many others with the fragrance of Christ by his very presence. To God be the glory.

Norm and Muriel Cook
First Taiwan missionaries
Multnomah School of the Bible

# Life – By a Fraction of an Inch

From *Unlock the Heavens*, Dick Hillis (Henderson, NE: Service Press), chapter 5, "Life – By a Fraction of an Inch"

The explosion made a shambles of our living room. Brick, broken glass and dirt covered the floor. Had the shot been a fraction of an inch higher, the entire family would have been wiped out. By a miracle, none was even injured. This was war, and in a war you expect some to be killed, especially when you are in the front lines. The twist in this story is that it was not our enemy but our friend who almost killed us.

Our well-built brick mission home sat right on the south bank of the Mule River. A small river, the Mule meandered slowly down through the province of Honan, joined the San River, and then flowed into the mighty Yellow River.

Right across the street from our home was the largest building in the town, a church built by the China Inland Mission. Nearly a thousand Christians worshiped here, coming in from surrounding villages to the marketplace to attend church on Sunday and to sell their produce during the week days.

Mule River Market looked like any of the thousands of Chinese towns. Main Street was cobbled with heavy marble stone, and the other streets were just mud or dust, depending upon the season. In the market square, garrulous Chinese farmers squatted on the ground, their produce spread out before them...carrots, sweet potatoes, soybeans, and wheat flour. Of course, you couldn't buy a television set, but you could buy dried scorpions, a very suitable medicine for any disease. And if you had eye trouble, an herb dealer might offer you powdered fingernails. During the market days we missionaries distributed Gospel tracts and preached to the curious crowds that gathered.

In peace time only a small civilian guard watched the gates of the Mule River Market village, but this was a time of civil war. For two years Mule River Market had been occupied by different sections of the Chinese Nationalist Army to protect it from the advancing Communist hordes. Soon after the Tenth Division arrived, I became acquainted with the artillery captain, a handsome young officer, who was proud of his halting English. Although I could not always decide whether he was speaking to me in English or Chinese, Captain Hwang and I soon became fast friends.

Captain Hwang was also proud of his big gun, which could lob a two-pound shell a mile and a half. He often boasted that he could stop any Communist with it. It was his dearest possession, and he cared for it like a teen-ager cares for his first car.

Early one December morning, Captain Hwang knocked on my door. When I opened it and invited him in, he began pacing the floor in an agitated manner and spoke to me excitedly.

"Honorable teacher, the Communists are marching on Mule River Market! It is possible they will reach the Market by nightfall and we will be in the midst of a hot war before the night is over!"

"What will be the outcome of the battle? Can you say, Captain?" I asked him, concerned for my family.

"You have nothing to fear. We can certainly take care of the

Communists with our brave men and our big guns. But I think you had better take your family and flee. Although we will never retreat, yet we expect this to be a dangerous battle."

It was impossible to flee. The Communists had blown up the railroad bridges both north and south of us.

Just after 9:00 p.m. we heard the first shot, and all night the battle increased intensely around us – a life and death struggle. Sleep was out of the question. We spent much of that night in prayer. By midnight the battlefield had shifted closer. Shots whistled through the air as men ran from one building to another. In the darkness we could see Nationalist soldiers on our neighbor's roof. Though I kept reminding myself that Christ had promised, "I will never leave thee, nor forsake thee" (Hebrews 13:5, KJV), I found myself tightening into a tense knot. I fought to keep calm but could hardly control my shaking. This was real war – house to house.

Unknown to us, a tiny gate in the city wall had been opened by our defending general. While his rear guard was fighting a delaying action, he and his men were slipping out across the river to a great walled city just a mile away. By daylight all was quiet, and we knew that our brave defenders had either surrendered or escaped.

When the sun arose, I took my first peek out of an upstairs window. The street was filled with soldiers, wearing red stars on their caps – soldiers of the Chinese Communist army! How long before they would discover us? Would they torture or kill us as they had done to some missionaries?

It was two days before the Reds seemed to discover us, but when they did, they treated us with a certain amount of courtesy. For 63 days we lived with this Communist army, and not a day lacked excitement. An order to stand trial before the Communist tribunal… a plea from the elder's wife to help get her jailed husband out of prison…a demand to find two guns buried by Nationalist soldiers on our property…several attempts by Communist officers to steal my jeep…a hundred seventy Christians living in the church and needing constant comfort and care…all of these events and more challenged our strength and faith.

One afternoon my old friend, Captain Hwang, added to the excitement. The whine of a shell and sudden explosion jolted Mule River Market and reminded us that Captain Hwang still believed his big guns could defeat the Communists. He had set up his artillery in the big city across the river, and was lobbing death into our streets. Unfortunately, he was killing more civilians than Communists. I could not tell him this. I could only pray that before the shells did any more damage he might tire of his deadly game of war.

As each shell dropped closer to our home, my wife and I realized that we must keep the children busy. To take their minds off the danger and noise we gathered them in the living room and suggested that they act out the famous Bible story found in the book of Esther. Children love to eat or just pretend they are eating, so they decided to play the feast scene. A hearty meal of water and crackers was prepared while the children chose their parts.

John, the eight-year-old, was made King Ahasuerus. Nancy, the six-year-old, was voted the prettiest and paraded around as Queen Esther. Seven-year-old Margaret volunteered to be the maid and set up the feast. Stephen, the youngest, was left with the unfortunate assignment of portraying Haman. The play moved on with dignity, and the sensational hanging took place when King John used Daddy's tie to fasten luckless Stephen by his neck to the back of a chair.

As the children were performing this gruesome act, a shell exploded just two doors from our house. I turned to my wife, "Margaret, keep the children busy. I'm going into the study to pray." The words had scarcely left my mouth when the next shell exploded in our yard, driving glass, bricks, and dirt into the very room where the children were playing. I shut my eyes in horror, expecting to find my children killed or injured when the dust cleared. But the next moment the four of them were clinging to my wife and me, crying hysterically. The explosion had shaken and momentarily deafened them. They were covered with dust but unharmed – not even a scratch could be found!

I gathered them up and we hid in the little room under the stairway. Would the next shell hit us? Would we reach Heaven together? Were we to meet death because of the act of a friend? I had little time to think. The next shell whined overhead and exploded in our neighbor's house, killing every member of the family. Brushing the tears from Nancy's eyes and the dust from her face, I tried to comfort her.

She looked up at me and, still sobbing and shaking, she said, "Daddy, I don't care if the next shell does hit us. Then we will go to Heaven and there aren't any shells in Heaven."

Taking strength from the thought of Heaven, I began to tell the children the story of Daniel.

"You know, we may meet Daniel tonight. John, what would you say to Daniel?"

John had been the first to stop crying. He said, with remarkable control, "I would tell him the same God Who took care of him in the lions' den took care of us in the war!"

Suddenly all was quiet. Captain Hwang had finished his little private war with the Communists. As we came out of our hiding place and looked at the room covered with bricks and sharp, death-dealing glass, I marveled that my children had come out of that room not only alive, but without a scratch or a bruise. God must have sent His angels to protect His little ones. Had these angels received the blows, deflected the flying glass and protected the children?

That night we shared a simple supper of soup and prepared our beds on the floor downstairs. The upstairs bedroom was too easy a target for Captain Hwang. We had much for which to be thankful – soup to eat, a floor to sleep on, and after all, weren't we alive, uninjured, and together?

After the children were tucked in bed, I came around to pray with each of them. As I knelt beside seven-year-old Margaret, I noticed a piece of paper tucked by her pillow. I looked closer. On this dirtied scrap of paper was printed in first-grade manner, "God is our refuge and strength, a very present help in trouble" (Psalm 46:1). Little Margaret was sleeping on a very big promise from a very big God. Whether friends or enemies were shooting at her, her confidence was in God.

The next morning I carefully examined the gaping hole made by the shell. Had Captain Hwang's gun been raised a tiny fraction of an inch, the shell would have exploded in the middle of the room in which the children were playing. This would have brought death to the entire family. Not only are the hairs of our heads numbered, but the very fraction of an inch is determined by Him Who said, "Fear thou not; for I am with thee: be not dismayed; for I am thy God: I will strengthen thee; yea, I will help thee; yea, I will uphold thee with the right hand of my righteousness" (Isaiah 41:10, KJV).

I do not know where Captain Hwang is today, but our four children are preparing to serve their Lord Who so graciously preserved them. They have learned that the minutest detail of life can be committed to a sovereign, loving God. They know that although we cannot always depend on men, whether they be friends or enemies, we can place our absolute confidence in God. He is in control of everything…down to the very fraction of an inch.

# THE STORIES I GREW UP WITH

The stories in this book are the ones I grew up with. Some of them came from Dad and Mother's earliest years in China, before I was born or while I was too young to remember. These are stories I heard Dad tell and retell, around the dinner table or at churches when we were in America on furlough.

Some of them I lived. In Loho, China, for example, I was in our little living room acting out the story of Esther with my brothers and sister when a shell exploded just outside our windows. From earliest memories I saw that Dad's life was so infused with purpose that personal survival was secondary to doing God's work and carrying His saving love to the people of China.

What a rich childhood I had, more exciting than Harry Potter, and, at the same time, deeply grounded in love! I learned to appreciate how special my dad's vision was, even compared to many missionaries of his generation. He brought no cultural imperialism to his task. He admired the high Chinese culture, but he was genuinely at home among the peasants of the countryside.

Dad couldn't be drawn into the rivalries of different denominations in building churches. He saw himself as a servant to the spiritual church—training evangelists and pastors and grounding new converts in the Bible.

Margaret Anne (Hillis) Pageler
Seattle, Washington

# My Communist Teacher

From *Unlock the Heavens*, Dick Hillis (Henderson, NE: Service Press),
chapter 6, "My Communist Teacher"

S now covered the muddy ground that Christmas night in 1947,
and the Prince of Peace seemed far from our little city of
Loho. The children were sound asleep, but I lay in bed fully
clothed and wide awake at 2:00 A.M. In the darkness I confessed to
Margaret that I couldn't help having the "shakes." Although God had
performed miracles for our family just a week before in preserving us
from injury when our house was struck by a shell, my mind was again
clouded with fear. Who knew what the next day might bring to us?
Torture or death?

At that very moment I was startled by a loud banging at the door
– made by the butt of a gun. This was it. I walked slowly downstairs
to the door. As I unlocked it, a soldier pushed by me, followed by
eleven of his men in disciplined file. Reaching the center of the room,
the leader swung around and I had my first good chance to look at
him.

He was about five feet eight inches tall and very thin. His
lieutenant's uniform was dirty, his shoulders slightly stooped. He had

a prominent chin, and his eyes held me – they looked as cold and hard as flint.

"Where does your wife sleep?"

"Upstairs."

"Tell her I'm using her bed – she can sleep on the floor."

"You can't do this," I bluffed. "I'm an American. This is my house and I order you to leave!" I wondered, as I spoke, if his heart were as hard as his eyes.

His hand went to his hip and drew a gun. "Get out!" he barked.

I obeyed, quickly moving my family to the little Chinese church across the street from the compound.

It was twenty eight days before I saw him again, this time at his invitation. He told me that within a week he would be leaving and I could have the house back. He assured me that I would find everything exactly as I had left it, for his men were honest and devoted Communists. Nothing would be stolen. As he talked, his eyes seemed softer, so I ventured a few questions.

"You say you are leaving in a week. Where are you going?"

"That's a military secret."

"How long have you been a Communist?"

"Two years."

Knowing the strength of family ties in China, I asked, "How long have you been away from home?"

"Fourteen months."

"And how old are you, sir?"

"Nineteen years old."

In China one is reckoned a year old when born, so that made him just eighteen.

"What do your parents do?"

"They are farmers in Shantung province."

"That worthy province was liberated by the Communists two years ago. I supposed your poor parents have received extra land and are better off now?"

"Not yet, but wait…the revolution is not over," he replied proudly. My questions had not even ruffled his confidence.

Four days later at dusk, the lieutenant again sent for me. I confess there was fear in my heart as I said good-bye to Margaret and walked across the street to the house we had once called our own.

The sight left me speechless. Lined up in perfect order were the soldiers who had been living in our house. The young lieutenant was searching their pockets. On the ground lay an old toothbrush, a tube of medical ointment (one of the men thought he had a new kind of toothpaste!), and a used razor.

As I watched, the lieutenant pulled a fork from the pocket of the soldier he was searching, slapped him across the face, and said, "We don't steal!"

When the inspection was over, he picked up the things and gave them to me, apologizing that his men had dared to steal. Then he ordered me to look through the house. It was filthy, but not a thing was missing. There was pride in his voice as he said, "I told you nothing would be stolen. Now go get your family because we are leaving tonight."

"Sir, may I ask you now where you are going?"

He answered by pointing to the high ancient walls of a city one mile away. I couldn't believe it.

"Do you realize there are ten thousand well-armed Nationalists there?"

"Yes, out intelligence knows all the figures," he replied.

"How many men in your group?" I asked him.

"We have nearly five thousand men who will take part in the attack," he answered.

"How many of them are armed, sir?"

"Two out of every three."

"You have a formidable enemy behind walls thirty feet high and fourteen feet thick," I told him. "Your enemy is not only well armed, but protected by a deep moat. You have only half the number of men. To attack that city is certain death."

As he listened to me, the young lieutenant straightened up and his eyes flashed fire. "We will take the city tonight or die trying."

"But, sir, has communism done anything for you? What have you gained from communism that would make you willing to lay down your life to carry it just one mile farther?"

"I fight not for personal gain," he replied fiercely. "It is what the world will gain that counts. I and my men are willing to die, if need be, but communism must win. The rule of my life is 'communism for all and my all for communism' – and 'all' includes death."

With that he swung on his heel, gave a sharp command, and he and his men disappeared into the night. Standing in the darkness, I asked myself the question, "Mr. Ambassador, you are an American with a great Christian heritage. Would you be willing to die to carry your message just one mile farther?"

The move into our house was a simple one. By ten that night the children were asleep. It was good to be back in our own home. With all safely in the house I slept soundly.

A terrific explosion blasted away my sleep! I lit a match and saw by my watch it was 2:30 A.M. The explosion had touched off the battle for the adjacent city. Nothing blocked our view of the city where the battle raged, sporadically lighted by the flashing of bursting shells. The horrible noise told a story of pain and death.

With the rising of the sun the firing ceased and men could be seen bearing the wounded on improvised stretchers. Had the Communists captured the city? It didn't seem possible. Had the lieutenant who had been willing to die for communism survived?

At 8:00 A.M. the remnants of the Red army retreated. That afternoon the commanding general of the Nationalist army came over to see us. He was amazed that we were alive and unharmed. I took him through our house and showed him where a shell in a previous battle had hit our living room and had come close to killing us all. I described the young Communist and asked about his company that had attacked the east gate.

"They didn't have a chance," he answered. "We had blown up the bridge across the moat. The Reds put down their scaling ladders and tried to crawl across, and we mowed them down like clay pigeons with our machine guns. The wounded drowned – it was slaughter! Not a man of that company escaped."

Though temporary peace had come, I couldn't sleep that night. In the moonlight I paced back and forth in our little yard. The Communist officer, now dead, kept speaking to me. His voice repeated: "I'll die, if need be, to carry communism one mile farther."

My heart trembled. Since 1933 I had been telling the great throbbing nation of China with its 400 million people that Christ revealed God's way of life and peace and salvation. The Communist lieutenant, fiery and dedicated, had also proclaimed a message: freedom from oppression through a people's government. He had been terribly deceived, but God had used him to teach me that I must have the urgency, the conviction, and the dedication that would make me a willing sacrifice for the success of my mission.

There in the moonlight I bowed my head and prayed, "Oh, God, make me willing to live, and die, if need be, to carry Your message of salvation one mile farther!"

# Part III
## Assignment China

"Every heart with Christ a missionary and
every heart without Christ a mission field."

# The Day the Dog Died

From *China Assignment*, Dr. Dick Hillis (Palo Alto, CA: Overseas Crusades, Inc., chapter 3, "The Day the Dog Died"

A woman's scream brought me out of deep sleep. I sat bolt upright in bed and was horrified to discover that the sky outside my window was a lurid red.

"*Tu-fei* (bandits)," whispered Mr. Kong, my Chinese teacher and traveling companion. "Hurry, we must run to escape!"

Shaking with fear, I pulled on my quilted gown. Kong unbarred the door and peered out into the village. "Follow me," he hissed. "We will try to make it to the wheat fields."

As we raced toward the fields, the noise of shooting, screaming, dogs barking, shouting men, and crackling flames filled the air. Not until we had put a comfortable distance between us and the village did we drop panting into the tall grain.

From our hiding place we watched the bandits plunder the village huts and then set fire to them. Few of the villagers tried to save their belongings but ran for their lives, as we did, for our Honan bandits were notorious for their vicious cruelty.

As we watched the holocaust, I recalled how indifferent these villagers had been earlier in the day as we told them of God's love for them. As I preached the crowd had pressed around me, but I knew their interest was more in my white face, blue eyes and big nose than in what I was saying.

"Yes, but if we burn our idols and worship the Supreme Emperor in heaven, who will placate the evil spirits?" they asked. "And if we do not burn incense for our ancestors, who will say prayers for us when we die?"

Being a farmer and understanding their fears, Kong answered their questions with a simple logic they could understand. Yes, the Gospel sounded like "happy news," they admitted, but no one dared to make the costly break.

"Yes, but…" – a dangerous phrase as I well knew. I myself had been guilty of this very mentality many times and it was my Chinese companion Kong who had taught me a lesson about this several weeks earlier.

Though Kong was only 22, he was a respected teacher in my area of China. He had finished eight years of school – quite an accomplishment in Honan in those days – to become certified as an elementary teacher.

It was at school where Kong first read a Bible. He found the "Holy" Book quite different from the sacred classics he had read and memorized. He started at Genesis and devoured the entire Old Testament in a few months. Then he came to John 10, "I am the Good Shepherd." Before going to school he had been a shepherd for his mother's small herd of goats so understood Christ's parable clearly. Suddenly he felt a great longing to meet this Good Shepherd.

The next Sunday Kong walked seven miles to church. That day Mr. Tomkinson, my senior missionary, had the joy of introducing him to the Good Shepherd.

When I arrived in Shenkiu, Kong became my language teacher. I found him to be the traditional Chinese gentleman – always polite and infinitely patient with me – so I nicknamed him "Little Confucius," the English way of saying "Teacher Kong."

Over the months he taught me a great deal more than the Chinese language. Although he came from a Buddhist home and had not attended Bible school, his faith was stronger than mine. He believed God's promises without a doubt and did not answer Him with a "Yes, but" as I often did. In fact, Kong's deep faith had startled me out of my "Yes, but" mentality several weeks earlier.

I was preaching to a crowd in a little village six miles north of the burning village when suddenly a man came running up and urgently whispered something to an elderly woman. Soon everyone began whispering to one another and I completely lost my audience.

Little Confucius stood up to politely restore silence when he was interrupted by a piercing scream, "*Chiu-ming* (save life)!" The entire crowd, including Kong and me, rushed down the street toward the house the scream had come from.

As we ran, Kong exclaimed, "I overheard that man say to the elderly lady that the spirits had arrived and a man was possessed!"

"That is wild superstition," I cautioned.

"But, Pastor, the Bible tells us that in Jesus' time men were possessed. Could not the same thing happen today?"

I started to answer Kong and stopped. Could it?

Crowding into a small courtyard, we could hear the sounds of struggling in the house and strained to see what was happening. Just then a distraught woman pushed her way through the villagers and came to Kong.

"The people say that you trust in the Supreme Emperor of heaven. I beg you to ask Him to help me! An evil spirit has again possessed the father of my children and is trying to kill him."

I could hardly believe it! The crowd parted for Kong and me as we moved toward the thatched hut. We stepped over a mangy brown and white dog that partially blocked the doorway and followed the little woman into a sparely furnished mud-walled room.

When my eyes adjusted to the dim light of a peanut oil lamp, on the bed I saw a middle-aged man held down by four other men. Although the prone man could not move his legs or arms, he was tossing his head wildly from side to side. Blood slowly oozed from a deep gash in his forehead – a wound that, we later learned, had been self-inflicted.

The atmosphere of the room seemed charged with evil, so real and close I felt I could lift my hand and touch it. My skin prickled with fear and nervousness.

To my relief, Little Confucius sized up the situation swiftly. First he addressed the family of the struggling man, "An evil spirit has possessed Farmer Ho. Our God, the 'Nothing-He-cannot-do One,' is bigger and more powerful than any spirit and He can deliver this man. First you must promise me you will burn your idols and trust in Jesus, the Son of this Supreme Emperor."

An old woman who was praying before the ancestral tablet in the corner raised her head in surprise, but no one spoke. Finally, one of the men nodded his assent. Later we learned he was Farmer Ho's younger brother.

Now turning to me Kong said, "You will sing with me three verses of the hymn, 'There is Power in the Blood.'"

Yes, of course, I believed that, but…!

"Would you o'er evil a victory win? There's wonderful power in the blood." Although neither of us could sing pleasingly, Farmer Ho grew calmer and so, I felt, did the atmosphere.

As we sang the last line of the hymn, II Corinthians 10:4 flashed into my mind, "For the weapons of our warfare are not carnal (physical), but mighty through God to the pulling down of strong holds." For the first time I was experiencing the forceful meaning of this verse, although I had memorized it at Biola several years ago.

Here in this little hut Kong and I were fighting a spiritual battle…a battle that Christ has won but we must claim. Swiftly, quietly I named each part of the "armor of God" and slipped them on by faith.

Kong took hold of my hand and said, "Now in the Name of Jesus we will command the evil spirit to leave this man."

Together we repeated, "In the mighty Name of Jesus we command you to come out of him!"

Did I honestly expect anything to happen? Kong obviously did for he began to pray fervently that every member of the Ho family would turn to God from idols and be saved.

He had just begun to pray when the dog let out a yelp as if someone had poured boiling water on its back. I turned and saw the poor animal whirling around in circles snapping wildly at his tail. The Ho family and I gazed in amazement, but Kong kept right on praying. Suddenly the dog fell over…dead!

I recalled Dr. Luke's eye witness account of the "devils that went out of the man, and entered into the swine: and the herd ran violently down a steep place into the lake, and were choked" (Luke 8:33, KJV). Had I witnessed something similar?

When Kong closed his prayer, Farmer Ho was quiet and relaxed. My teacher asked the family to fix the resting man some chicken broth. While the wife set about preparing the chicken Kong began to teach the family more about Jesus.

Two weeks later, the Ho family burned their idols and their ancestral tablet and became Christians. When Mr. Ho was baptized he testified, "I was possessed by an evil spirit who boasted he had already killed five people and was going to kill me. He would have accomplished his boast, but God sent Mr. Kong along just at the right moment and in Jesus' Name I was set free."

And that is how Little Confucius taught me that the "Yes,

but…" mentality would offer only defeat in both the Christian walk and warfare. Even in the fiercest battle the way to sure victory is an *unqualified* "Yes" to God.

# CONSIDER THIS TRIP A FAILURE

During almost fifty-one years with OC, Dick Hillis has been our very favorite missionary statesman and mission director. He has always been a perfect example and used his gifts to faithfully serve the Lord.

I'll never forget the very first Venture for Victory (now called Sports Ambassadors) basketball team sent to Taiwan in 1952. Dick was outside of the office in Taipei, giving our team an introduction to the country, the people, and the expected ministry. He said, as he tipped his chair back, "We're mighty glad you're here, but if some of you don't return as missionaries, I'm going to consider this trip a failure." The audacity!

Because OC was a mission that used the unorthodox approach of basketball to win people to Christ, and God had given me the ability to play basketball, it was very logical to me to go overseas as a missionary. Consequently, our family served twelve years in the Philippines and then three years in Australia. The teams that were organized and sent out saw many hundreds of thousands of those basketball-crazy Filipinos ministered to. Many trusted the Savior.

We will be eternally grateful the Holy Spirit used him to be such a faithful servant and have such an influence in our lives and the lives of so many. He put steel in our souls.

Bud Schaeffer
Sports Ambassadors

# The Impossible Mission

From *China Assignment*, Dr. Dick Hillis (Palo Alto, CA: Overseas
Crusades, Inc., chapter 4, "The Impossible Mission"

"Please come to my home and help me burn my idols. I want to
become a Christian."

This cry for help from Mr. Lin, a poor, illiterate Chinese
farmer, brought great rejoicing to my heart because it was addressed
to another Chinese farmer, a Christian named Ma. Would Mr. Ma
now prove the truth of the formula for missionary success God had
given me several weeks earlier?

Ever since arriving in China's inland province of Honan, I had
been depressed by the very impossibility of my task as a missionary.
How could one man reach a million and a half people with the Gospel?
The few dozen Christians in the area knew nothing about preaching.
Besides, they were too busy working their small farms and providing
for their large families. To help me with my impossible mission I had
only Mr. Kong, abiding Chinese evangelist.

True, I did not have trouble attracting crowds in the villages Mr.
Kong and I visited. The word that a foreigner was in the village quickly
spread from hut to hut and soon the marketplace would be crammed
with curious men, women, and children, all interested in examining

my blue eyes and touching my white skin. And just to be sure that no one stayed away, I would take my trumpet and play one of the eleven hymns I had memorized.

In spite of my inexperience, I knew I must keep my messages simple. Often I would begin by drawing the crowd's attention to the Chinese character for "come." This character is made of a cross with two little men hanging on the ends of its outstretched arms. In the center hangs a larger man. From this symbol it was not difficult to explain the meaning of the crucifixion.

Then I would repeat the Savior's loving invitation, "Come unto me, all ye that labor and are heavy laden, and I will give you rest" (Matthew 11:28, KJV). Surely, I reasoned, these hard-working farmers could understand this verse.

When I ran out of vocabulary, young Kong would preach. His messages were more personalized than mine, for he had been raised in Honan and knew the superstitions and fears of even the most ardent idol worshipper. Using careful logic, he would try to lead his listeners from the false gods they knew to the one true God they did not know. But in spite of his earnest appeals and my simple messages, all too few responded to the Gospel of Christ.

After several months of this exhausting schedule, the futility of my task began to eat at me. At this rate I would never reach even a fraction of Honan's multitude. I had expected God to shower His supernatural power upon my ministry. What was wrong?

During these trying months I had trouble sleeping. I can remember turning and twisting on my hard cot many nights after Kong had been asleep for several hours. Our little mud hut always seemed unusually dark and close these troubled nights, and the greedy, whining mosquitoes that fought their way through my net added to my discomfort.

If this were the glamor of missionary service I wanted no more of it. If those ladies in the missionary societies at home could have read my thoughts now how disillusioned they would be in their successful young missionary.

One hot, stuffy, airless night, as I lay staring into the darkness, a familiar Scripture verse crossed my mind, "And He saith unto them, Follow me and I will make you fishers of men" (Matthew 4:19).

I tried but could not dismiss the words from my mind, "Follow me and I will make you fishers of men." The twelve disciples followed Jesus wherever He went, learning how to preach from Him. I had no one following me. Was my message right but my method wrong?

As this new and exciting possibility hit me I lost all desire for sleep. I pushed my net aside, lit the little peanut oil lamp, and opened my Bible. "Ye shall be witnesses," Jesus said in Acts 1:8. To whom was He speaking? To the disciples gathered around Him at His ascension. *And* to the handful of Christians in Shenkiu...the farmers, the merchants, and the housewives!

Reading on in Acts 20:4, I discovered that Paul also used this method of evangelism. Yes, I had been using the wrong formula. I had tried to evangelize the world by myself. Tomorrow would bring some startling changes!

Kong awakened just as the rooster crowed outside our little hut and was puzzled to see me already dressed and rolling up my bed bag.

"You must be anxious to be on your way. I certainly hope we have more success today than yesterday!"

"I am not preaching today," I replied. "I am going back to Shenkiu."

"But, *Heh-muh-si* (Pastor Hillis), you mustn't give up so easily!" Kong argued, and, thinking I was discouraged, tried to comfort me.

I explained that I would not preach again until the believers went out with me. He was convinced I was merely depressed, so we walked back to the city in silence.

The next Sunday morning in our little Shenkiu chapel my text was Acts 1:8, "Ye shall be witnesses." I asked the farmers in the congregation to stay behind after the service. When they gathered around me, I told them what I wanted:

"Harvesting will be completed in several weeks. Then you will have nearly a month of free time before you can plant your next crop. During your slack time I want you all to go out into the villages and witness with me."

Mr. Ma (or Horse) interrupted me excitedly, "But, *Heh-muh-si,* how can I preach when I have only a third grade education?"

"You can read," I replied, "and as a Christian farmer you can tell unbelieving farmers what Jesus Christ means to you."

Now the questions came fast.

"But if we are gone for a month what will we eat?"

"How much will you pay us?"

"We don't even know how to witness. How can we learn?"

"One at a time," I laughed, "We will eat the same things you would eat at home but we will carry it with us. As for salary, well, turn to your Bibles and if you can find how much Jesus paid Peter and John I will give you the same amount! And you will learn to witness by following me."

The farmers were skeptical of my plan but they agreed to give it a try. We closed with a short prayer meeting and a promise to meet again on Monday, October 25.

In spite of their doubts the Christians who gathered at the little church on October 25 were eager to begin their training as witnesses for Christ. Each one brought with him a sack of flour or a basket of soy beans to be used as our food staples for the month. No sleeping bags were necessary, as we slept on straw spread on the mud floor of the church.

For the next month we followed a disciplined schedule. Every day at 5:00 a.m. we pulled on our long quilted gowns and cotton wadded trousers and took time for individual prayer and Bible study. At seven we breakfasted on steaming hot flour-and-water gruel. Then back to Bible study and evangelism training. About nine-thirty, young Kong, the elected captain of the group, sent the men out two by two. Every day I accompanied a different team of men.

When we entered the village marketplaces I would let the Chinese Christians tell the great love story.

"Come and hear the Good News," they would call.

"Down with your false gods and your idol worship. You worship the god of peace, and you and your mate fight like roosters. Is it not so? You worship the god of wealth, and has he made any of you rich? Are you not almost starving to death? You worship the goddess of health, and sickness walks in and out your front door. I urge you to turn to Jesus!"

"Who is this Jesus?" the villagers wondered. "How do you turn to Him and what happens if you do? And what is the Good News? Nothing these strangers from Shenkiu say sounds very good! Oh, well, it is an interesting diversion from the day's work!"

At dusk each day the teams returned to the church to rest hoarse throats and tired bodies and to share the experiences of the day. At first, their experiences were not very encouraging. Even though I went with a different team each day and when my turn came I told the villagers very clearly of the life, miracles, death and resurrection of Christ, the Christians with me seemed slow to realize that *their* preaching contained no "Good News."

It was the afternoon Mr. Lin asked Mr. Ma to come to his home and burn his idols that things began to happen. That day Mr. Ma finally saw the importance of preaching the Good News. As the simple story of God's grace unfolded from his lips, the Spirit of God revealed to Mr. Lin his need of the Savior.

"You *must* help me find the true God," he begged.

He had no way of knowing the fear and excitement his request raised in Mr. Ma's heart, and the rejoicing in mine!

Mr. Ma and Mr. Chang, his teammate, went home with Mr. Lin and explained to the family, "If you would worship the true God you must rid your home of the false."

Together they took down the ancestral tablet, two paper gods, a clay kitchen god and an incense bowl. With an air of triumph the men carried the idols outside and smashed and burned them. Then the little family knelt in prayer with the two Chinese Christians.

Back at the church that night, Ma and Chang could not hide their enthusiasm. "The Gospel is the power of God, even when *we* preach it!"

Their enthusiasm was catching, and the little group of men suddenly saw that a farmer could win a farmer. Now the days were not long enough as the Christians discovered how readily the villagers would accept the *Good News* from their lips. Then we ran out of food. Would God use ravens to feed the team as He did Elijah? No, He did not, so the team members returned to their homes and farms.

"But we will be back as soon as the sweet potatoes are harvested!" they promised, and they were!

This was the beginning of the Gospel's sweep across our thickly populated country. Calling themselves "The Gospel Workers' Team," the Shenkiu Christians traveled from village to village witnessing to their rural neighbors. Soon a similar women's team was born. In the next five years so many new churches were formed that the elders of our Shenkiu church went to different villages every Sunday so each new group of believers could hold the communion service at least once a month.

By following the formula of "every Christian a witness," the Chinese believers of Shenkiu accomplished the impossible mission.

# Part IV
# Not Made for Quitting

"Build a platform for the younger men."

# Don't Interfere with My Plans

From *Not Made for Quitting*, Dr. Dick Hillis (Minneapolis, MN: Dimension
Books, 1973), chapter 2, "Don't Interfere with My Plans"

**Bud Schaeffer**
*Little All-American basketball player
Coach of Venture for Victory basketball team
Coach of Chinese Olympic Team in 1956
Missionary with Overseas Crusades, Inc.
in the Philippines and Australia)*

W ould God ask him to give up basketball? Bud tried to put
the nagging question out of his mind as he dribbled the
ball across the court. He hollered to some of his teen-
age chums. They trotted over to shoot baskets with the school's star
cager.

Their noisy comradeship only temporarily drowned the battle
Bud Schaeffer was fighting. Was he willing to surrender completely
to God?

By all normal standards, Bud ran his own life successfully enough.
His high school buddies voted him junior class vice president, senior
class president, president of the hundred-voice glee club, and "most
likely to succeed." He spent his stint with the Navy playing basketball
on their Great Lakes squad against Big Ten schools.

In college he led his class during his freshman and senior years as president and for four years was chosen for the All-Conference basketball team. Little All-American honors and a year of pro-ball followed. There was no question about Bud's ability on his own.

But God had early laid claim to Schaeffer's life. Would Bud yield God everything, even his love for basketball and his yen for a machinist's career?

As a youngster, Bud Schaeffer was torn between the ways of his father and his mother. Bud's mother regularly took her children to a Gospel Tabernacle where Beryl, Bud's older sister, became his Sunday school teacher. Mr. Schaeffer lost five houses to the bank during the depression. Being a bartender, he had access to a quick cure for all his woes, and Bud saw him drunk more often than sober.

Bud ran around with a gang of junior high boys who vaunted their maturity, as boys do, by smoking and by committing acts of impudent vandalism. Following his dad's example, young Schaeffer used to stay up all night gambling. Then on Sundays he had to go to church with his mother and Beryl, where he would squirm through Sunday school and the morning service.

He was thirteen when the preaching of the Word hit home. As conviction deepened, he knew he must make his decision. But what would his friends think? When the invitation was given, with characteristic courage, Bud went straight to the altar to put his trust in Christ.

"As I walked out of that meeting," Bud recalls, "it seemed like the angels were singing right above my head. I had accepted Jesus Christ and He had accepted me."

Then tragedy struck. Bud's mother died. The sudden disaster brought his bartender father to his senses, and he was wonderfully converted and surrendered his life to God.

"Both my dad and I were looking for satisfaction at the wells of this world," Bud explains, "and we always went away thirsty until we drank of the Water of Life, Christ Himself."

Though Bud accepted Christ's salvation, he had some reservations about Christ's control. Bud wanted to play basketball and to be a machinist. Did dying to self mean giving up the ball court and the machine shop? Let Bud describe his conflict:

"I felt that God would have me go into the ministry, but I never told anyone. For two years I had a tremendous struggle in my heart. To me, going into the ministry was the most difficult thing I could imagine! I had over 1500 hours of high school machine shop work to my credit, and I didn't want the Lord to interfere with my plans.

"My prayers went something like this: 'Lord, I don't seem to be willing to do absolutely anything You want, but I pray that You'll make me willing. If necessary Lord, even knock me down on the flat of my back and cause me to die if I'm not willing, but somehow, make me willing.'

"With boyish practicality, I was pretty sure God would never take such drastic measures. While I was in the Navy at the age of eighteen, after hearing a message that wasn't even about dedication, I slipped out of my seat and yielded my life for the ministry."

That act of surrender rang the curtain on Bud's machine shop work, but his basketball career was still in Act One. At Wheaton College, Bud's prowess on the court kept his fans constantly amazed. "Unbelievable Bud" they called him.

When Bud had the ball no one could keep him away from the basket. Confronted with an opponent, one of his favorite tricks was to break his dribbling pace and send a high bounce over the man's head. Round the startled player he swooped to catch the ball on the jump and toss it through the hoop in one swift motion. Sometimes he would slam it against the backboard, catch it going full speed and shoot while still in the air. But more than being a "ball hog," he was a sparkplug for teamwork.

The pro teams made bids for Bud's services when he graduated, and Schaeffer spent a high-speed year on a team called the Boston Whirlwinds (now Celtics) playing exhibition ball against the world-famous Harlem Globetrotters team in forty different states and Cuba.

In the one game that the Whirlwinds defeated the Globetrotters out of the fifty or so games they played against them, Bud got one-third of his team's points when they won, 51 to 47, in Havana, Cuba.

Afterwards the owner and coach of the Globetrotters, Abe Saperstein, asked Schaeffer to be a member of the United States All Stars which was to tour South America for nine weeks, playing against the Globetrotters. Bud reminded Abe that if he did he would not play on Sunday. Saperstein still insisted that he go.

Bud married talented, artistic Alice Brown one week later, and after a two-week honeymoon he flew to South America to begin the tour. While in Rio de Janeiro, Brazil, the teams played before fifty thousand people at one game, up to that time the largest paid attendance to witness a basketball game. While the team was in Buenos Aires, Argentina, President Juan Peron and his beautiful wife, Eva, went to the game at Luna Park Stadium.

Immediately afterwards the Perons gave a cocktail party for the teams. Due to his convictions about drinking, Bud remained outside the room passing out Gospel tracts to the policemen sent there to guard their leaders.

After half an hour, Eva Peron emerged and saw Bud standing outside in his shiny yellow-orange uniform. She extended her hand to him. Just that morning, Bud had read, "I will speak of thy testimonies also before kings, and will not be ashamed" (Psalm 119:46, KJV). Reaching into this jacket pocket he pulled out a tract in Spanish, "Five Things God Wants You to Know."

As Madame Peron received it, she said in Spanish, "Oh, do you want my autograph?"

Schaeffer said in Spanish, "No, this is for you."

"Oh, thank you!"

As she went out the door, Bud prayed that her woman's curiosity and the Holy Spirit would not let her rest until she read it carefully. Later Bud learned that just the day before she had spoken to hundreds of thousands of people in Buenos Aires and millions more on the radio, saying, "My husband Juan is god. Heaven would not be heaven without my husband. He is the very air we breathe." One year later she died of cancer.

Now it was time to give up basketball and prepare for the ministry. Bud enrolled at Fuller Seminary. His first year he was chosen president of his class.

In 1950 Bud toured Europe as song leader and soloist on a Gospel team. In the summer of 1952, Coach Don Odle asked Bud to travel with the first Venture for Victory basketball team to the Orient. As well as for their playing ability, members are chosen for their Christian experience and musical and speaking abilities.

Schaeffer states: "I'm thankful that in 1950 I had the hottest night I ever had on a basketball court the last game of my Wheaton College career when we played Taylor University. I was able to hit eleven of twelve long shots from the middle of the court. No doubt this was one big reason (if not the main reason), other than my Christian testimony, that Coach Don Odle asked me to join the rest of the Taylor team that first year out to the Orient."

Still Bud had no intention of being a foreign missionary. He had yielded his life to the Lord for full-time ministry, and it was up to God to show him where that ministry should be. The Venture for Victory summers of 1952 and 1953 cinched the answer to Bud's old question. Did God want him to give up sports? No, God intended him to use his basketball ability as a wedge to open doors to the Gospel in the Far East.

Basketball had never been tried to the extent the first Venture for Victory team planned to use it for evangelism. No one on the team or those arranging the schedule knew whether or not it would work. Most of the games and meetings were planned for the island bastion of Formosa. Preachers or missionaries could not gain entrance into the schools and army camps for evangelistic purposes, but since basketball was the number one game, a team from the United States was very welcome. That first summer the team played eighty-seven games. It was not unusual for over two hundred soldiers, sailors, air force men, or students to remain after the game, bow their heads and ask Christ to forgive their sins.

Often the team played three games a day, even with some players sick because of the heat, food, water, or travel. But Bud says he will never forget the joy of lying down at night and realizing that that day hundreds of precious souls had opened their hearts to the Savior on the basketball courts. He and the team looked forward to every game. They were constantly amazed at the ways basketball opened up doors for the Gospel.

Now located in the Philippines, the 180-pound six-foot athlete scores high with the Orientals. Bud and Alice sometimes team up together in singing and witnessing, Alice with her colored chalk and singing ministry. Schaeffer witnesses to God's saving power with all the drive and enthusiasm that made him a professional ball player. A wide grin slashes his angular face as he presents Christ to a pedicab driver, a college professor, or a teen-age sports fan.

"Basketball evangelism" is our name for the kind of work Bud does. In ten years of missionary service Bud played over six hundred games. Each one gives opportunities for preaching at half time and personal counseling later. Basketball clinics get Schaeffer into high schools as short-term coach.

For four months in 1956, Overseas Crusades loaned Schaeffer to the Chinese Nationalist Olympic Committee, which was preparing their teams for the Olympics in Melbourne, Australia. Coaching the Chinese basketball squad was exciting work.

"Lots of spring in those legs. Head up. Follow through! Good! Watch the wrist action next time," coaches Schaeffer, catching the ball as it swishes through the net and sending it back with a bounce to the keyhole where little Mr. Chu, Chinese All-Star, is perfecting his free-throw technique.

The next ball teeters on the rim, then drops beside the basket. "You're tired," laughs Bud, retrieving the ball.

"And hot," admits Chu, wiping his forehead. In the humid, tropical summer the cotton uniforms of both men stick to their damp skins.

Schaeffer reaches for a bottle opener and opens two bottles of "Aerated Water," the popular Formosan soft drink. The two men sit on the first rung of the empty bleachers and talk over the prospects of the coming game.

"Want to work on that one hand jump shot?" asks Schaeffer, depositing the two empty bottles in the case. But Chu is glad to have the coach alone for a minute. Something has been puzzling him.

"Mr. Schaeffer, Sir, I don't understand what you are doing in the Orient. With your ability, you could be playing pro-ball or coaching in a Big Ten school in the States. You could make money – lots of it. Out here you coach us for nothing. It doesn't make sense to me."

Bud's eyes sparkle with anticipation. He knows Chu well enough by now to know just where to meet him. "You are a jet pilot, Mr. Chu. What kind of flying do you do?"

Mr. Chu tells of the twenty missions he has flown over Red China to drop leaflets encouraging the Chinese people to retain their hope for freedom.

"Were those missions dangerous?" asks Bud.

"Sure," admits Chu, "but national freedom is more important than personal safety."

"That's how I feel too," says Schaeffer. "Some things are more important than personal ambition." He proceeds to tell Chu the story of Jesus Christ's death for him.

Chu's dark eyes moisten as the cruelty of the crucifixion takes hold of his heart, and he responds with a barely-repressed shout to the glory of the resurrection. For the first time the old, old story means something to him. It is told him by a man he can trust, by a man whose whole life is a testimony to its practical power.

"Mr. Schaeffer, could you teach me how to be a Christian?" asks Chu after a pause.

Bud's smile seems to say, "Sure, man, that's just what I am here for."

Schaeffer's enthusiastic letters record spiritual victories as well as athletic, "A team member, small Mr. Chu, a jet pilot with twenty missions over Red China, accepted the Lord last week...others have expressed interest. Pray with me."

In another letter the Olympic coach writes, "The basketball team manager, Captain Tang, received Christ as his personal Savior yesterday. He came to church to hear me speak, and at the invitation came forward for Christ."

Most of the year Bud's missionary work in the Philippines is much the same as that of any other missionary. He is active in Bible classes, city-wide crusades, pastors' and laymen's conferences, and the ever-present opportunities in personal evangelism to point prepared men, women and youth to Christ.

But the summers are different. When June rolls around, Schaeffer moves his field of witness to the basketball court.

For ten summers Bud has played with the Venture for Victory team. This has taken him to fourteen countries of the Orient and has given him opportunity to witness to around five million people who, no doubt, would not have come under the hearing of the Gospel in any other way.

Bud never limits his witness to the half-time program. With heart and mind full of the Word, he maneuvers to instant witness whenever the Holy Spirit indicates the opportunity. With Schaeffer, witnessing involves not only words but life and attitude. Many times on the basketball court I have watched him answer a dirty play or a purposeful foul from his opponent with a smile. Bud never forgets that his vocation is witnessing for Christ. To him basketball is a delightful avocation that enables him to more completely accomplish his vocation.

When the Venture for Victory team does not go to the Orient, Bud gets together with a team of missionaries. The majority of the Crusaders team, as they call themselves, is made up of Venture for Victory alumni, men who were sent to play and stayed to preach.

Conditions under which the men play would be enough to make most men hang up their suits, but Schaeffer insists, "Circumstances become immaterial to us when we have the chance to talk to a spectator or a cager about Christ."

"Play in the rain?" Of course! At one game, while the players slid from one end to another, the referee trotted up and down the court with a whistle in one hand and an umbrella in the other. At another game, Schaeffer helped dig small trenches to draw the water off the dirt court. Then, let her rain – the game must go on.

One court had the main road running across it, so every few minutes the whistle blew to give a logging truck temporary right of way. When the lights went out at one night game, the motorcycle police beamed their headlights at the team so they could continue their half-time preaching to the 3,000 spectators.

When I asked Bud why he was in the Orient, he answered my question by relating a personal experience:

"I was in a solemn communion service in the States where more than 1500 Christians were present. The elements were passed out and then the pastor asked, 'Is there anyone who has been omitted?' A missionary from India stood and said, 'Four hundred fifty million in India have been omitted.' A moment of hush was broken when a missionary from the Philippines stood, 'Thirty million of our people have been omitted.'

"This continued for some time as missionaries from different countries told of vast populations omitted from the Lord's salvation because no one had told them of Jesus Christ, the Way. Christ's death on Calvary was as much for them as for me and as long as God wants me to use a basketball to attract them and a BOOK to win them, I will do His will.

"And when God tells me to pass the ball on to somebody else and just use the Book, I will hang up my suit and be obedient."

# GO AND PREACH THE GOSPEL!

Don and I have been richly blessed by the life and spirit of Dick Hillis, beginning in 1952 when the first Venture for Victory (Sports Ambassadors) basketball team went to Taiwan at the invitation of Dick and Madame Chiang Kai-shek. Don and the team had little idea of what they were getting into, but the dedication and leadership of Dick Hillis and the OC people was what God used to introduce the gospel to thousands of people. We had the privilege of seeing for the first time a missionary in action in a foreign land and people responding to the Good News of Jesus Christ, our Savior.

It was my privilege to be in the Hillis home in Taiwan in 1953 and then to have the joy of having Dick in our home many times in Upland, Indiana, where he shared the challenge of missions with the Taylor University student body. God used Dick Hillis in Don's and my life to challenge us to "go and preach the gospel," and we had the joy of doing that for many years through the basketball ministry.

Don and Bonnie Odle
Former OC board member
Coach, Venture for Victory, '52-'66

# The Battle of the Talented

From *Not Made for Quitting*, Dr. Dick Hillis (Minneapolis, MN: Dimension Books, 1973), chapter 11, "The Battle of the Talented"

**Norman Nelson**
*Missionary with Overseas Crusades*
*Tenor Soloist*
*Singing Ambassador at Large*

"Singing Ambassador" is no mere public relations title for Norman Nelson. He has sung in vast arenas and in the private chambers of presidents. His powerful tenor voice has filled the public squares of town and hamlets in a dozen outlands.

He has sung in person before audiences totaling more than three million in the Orient, and his magnificent tenor voice is recognized and loved by thousands more who hear him daily on the radio.

"We are Christ's ambassadors," is the message of Norm's songs. "God is using us to speak to you: we beg you, as though Christ Himself were here pleading with you, receive the love He offers you" (II Corinthians 5:20, *Living Letters*). And the vibrant operatic tenor rolls forth a verse of "There Is No Greater Love" or "It's Real, I Know It's Real."

Testimonies to the reconciling work accomplished in the hearts of many listeners fill Norm's mail box. "I will always thank and praise

God for sending you to Davao City," writes a Filipino girl. "You know, sir, every member of my family received the Lord through the message in your wonderful songs."

Norm's own life was transformed by the message of a song, one which he himself was singing. Singing was the thing he like best to do as a child, and Sunday school and church provided him with an abundant repertoire. He was singing to himself one day when he realized that the words of the chorus were meant for him. "Come into my heart, Lord Jesus," he sang, making it his own prayer and in that instant received new life as a son of God.

Since the age of thirteen, then, Norm has belonged to God, but throughout his high school and college days again and again he faced the question of how best to use his growing talent. As a result of Norm's excellent portrayal of Faust in a high school performance of Verdi's Opera, his music teacher offered him a scholarship to study for a career in opera. Norm was already being coached by the leading operatic tenor in Denver and was invited to audition for the Jack Benny show. With his dynamic voice and winning stage presence, Norm was a natural for a career in professional entertainment.

But once again a song gripped his heart and transposed his life. One Sunday evening as a college quartet sang at his church, Norm heard God's call to full-time Christian service and vowed to use his voice always in consonance with the glory of his Lord. His musical training then took on added seriousness, as he realized that his vocal skill could amplify or deaden the impact of the words he sang.

But the sacrifices were real ones. From the glamor of a professional career, Norm and his pert wife Georgia turned to the hardships of financial and geographical insecurity. Norm worked as Youth for Christ director, as minister of visitation, as singer on evangelistic teams, and as pastor. After over a dozen moves in ten years, the Nelsons and their little children finally settled down in a home which Norm, contrasting it to some of the parsonages and apartments they had known, describes as having "wall-to-wall floors."

At this point God introduced a new theme, running contrary to the growing security of the young pastor. Norm was suddenly confronted by the challenge of missions. Already a dedicated minister, disciplined to a life of sacrificial obedience, surely the decision would be easy for him. But no. He faced several real obstacles.

"At best I had a distorted picture of missionaries and missions in general. Although I had pastored two different churches, missions to me was a charitable enterprise to which we donated our funds each year. And to be truthful, our incentive in giving to missions was the desire to be up towards the top in our district as a church. Since none of the other churches did very much for missions, we were third or fourth from the top, although we gave only $1,200 a year from a church with 250 active members."

In the summer of 1955, a trip to the Orient opened Norm's eyes. With an evangelist and chalk artist, he toured Japan, Formosa, and the Philippines, singing in school assemblies, village plazas, and city auditoriums. People by the thousands came to listen, particularly in the Philippines, where the cordial American with his resonant voice was an immediate hit. The impact of his singing, coupled with the genuine and eager response of the people to the Gospel, woke Norm up.

Scenes from the tour nagged Norm that fall. Should he continue a ministry in the States when such an arpeggio of opportunity awaited in the Orient? When he received an invitation from Overseas Crusades to serve in the Philippines for two years, Norm took it as God's downbeat. But there was a second snag.

Georgia Nelson had not gone on that summer tour. She had stayed in America expecting their fourth child and, for the first time in ten years, enjoying a measure of security. Norm had a good position in a fine church, with invitations to sing almost every evening throughout the Los Angeles area. They had purchased a home of their own, and some of the furniture was already paid for. They had even arranged financing for a brand new automobile after years of struggling with mechanical has-beens.

"Could God really ask them to break up housekeeping and start all over again?" Georgia wondered.

Knowing feminine psychology, Norm soon capitulated to his wife's arguments, saying soothingly, "Honey, you are absolutely right. This measure of security is God's gift to us. We should be grateful for it and not even consider leaving it to go to the mission field."

"Now wait a minute," Georgia objected, and gave her husband a little sermon about the importance of obeying God no matter what the cost.

For two days Norm played obstinate. As he tells the story, "Georgia preached to me with such fervor during those two days that she herself was convinced without a shadow of a doubt that this was what God wanted for us." With a roguish grin he adds, "You should have seen the mixture of triumph and vexation on her face when I told her I'd been determined to go all along!"

Once their hearts were in tune with each other and with God's will, Norm and Georgia's material ties unraveled more easily than they had imagined.

"It is amazing," says Norm, "How the things that seem so precious to you can suddenly become so much excess baggage. Believe it or not, we were thrilled when finally the real estate man told us the house was sold. We were able to sell all our furniture and get rid of our car. Within three months we had been given a new station wagon for our work on the field, our support and passage money was raised and we were ready to go."

Oh, the thrill of using a God-given talent to its full capacity...the delight of singing the Gospel to eager, attentive crowds...the deep satisfaction of following up genuine conversions. Norm and Georgia had known nothing like it in their American ministry.

Norm teamed up with Filipino evangelist Greg Tingson and began a crusade ministry that saw over thirty thousand respond to Gospel invitations during Nelson's first four years in the Philippines.

"We met in the plaza of one Muslim community," writes Norm, describing a typical meeting. "As the evening service began we stood on the makeshift platform. First of all, I gave a concert. Then Greg Tingson preached a dynamic Gospel message. Rarely have I seen a more attentive audience.

"In this Muslim area where during an entire campaign usually only one or two will care to publicly acknowledge Christ as Savior, we were astonished to see thirty step forward. To some of these it will mean persecution, being disowned by their families, and even the threat of death."

But it takes more than an overseas location to make a missionary... more than a charming cordiality and a magnetic voice. The missing ingredient was one which Norman Nelson sought for a long time.

"I didn't have a burden for the lost," he admits. "I didn't love my neighbor. I didn't have a real desire to see him won. I prayed for this love. I tried in many ways to gain the same burden for souls that caused John Knox to cry, 'Give me Scotland or I die.' Yet I had to be honest with myself: the concern just wasn't there. What was wrong with me? I prayed. I read my Bible. I tried and tried.

"Then God spoke to me through Romans 6:13. I realized that in order to have a burden for the lost I would have to see them through God's eyes, not my own. 'Yield your members as instruments of righteousness unto God.' Surely an instrument does not try to play itself. As long as I tried to drum up my own emotions I was out of step with God. But when I yielded myself as an instrument God produced His own harmony."

"If you want a burden for the lost," says Norm from his own

experience, "if you want to become a missionary, allow God to make you His own instrument. God's eyes see each man compassionately, knowing and hating his sinfulness, but providing and desiring his salvation. When I become God's tool, I no longer see my neighbor through self-centered eyes, but I see him as God sees him – with a redemptive purpose in mind.

"Now as I stand in the market place of an Oriental town, absorbing the unique sights and smells and sounds, there is a deep compassion within my heart. I look out on a plaza filled with sinful human beings, whose hearts know fear and failure, guilt and grief, and I feel something of what Jesus must have felt as He looked over the city of Jerusalem and cried, 'How often I have wanted to gather your children together' (Matthew 23:37, *Living Gospels*)."

Another obstacle Norm faced he named "the battle of the talented." But God gave him grace to play the right chord.

"If God will not share His glory with another," says Norm, "then God and I will not get glory from the same performance. I soon learned that you cannot at one and the same time show how great you are and how wonderful your Lord is. The choice is not a once-for-all proposition, but rather a day-by-day experience. Each day I simply ask God to let me sing for *His* glory."

Norm admits that even after becoming a foreign missionary he had his problems, the toughest one being the inferiority complex he developed about being "just a missionary." Like most missionaries Norm finds it necessary to travel a great deal. So now we see him on a sleek jet liner. Seated next to him is a sharp up-and-coming young executive. Soon they are in conversation.

After the young businessman has explained his work, he turns to Norm and says, "And, by the way, what's your line?"

"I would put on my best smile," Norm says, "look him right in the eye, and reply, 'I'm a missionary.' Suddenly a startled expression would come across his face. I could almost hear the wheels turning in his mind as he said to himself, 'Oh, no, a real live one right here beside me.' Then an amazing transformation would take place. The stark expression of amazement would change to a far-off, visionary expression and, looking out into space, he would say in a pious tone, 'My, that's a wonderful calling!'

"He didn't mean a word of it. It was a poor cover up. All the time he was thinking, 'This poor monk, living off the hills, doesn't know what life is all about.' After many such encounters a mounting inferiority complex began to build in my mind and I would say to myself, 'This man is in big business, but I am just a missionary!'"

I am going to let Norm tell you how God took care of this problem: "One of my missionary journeys took me to M'Lang, Cotabato, on the island of Mindanao in the Philippines. This is a pioneer town, much like the days of the Old West here in the United States. The people are homesteaders who have come from everywhere in the Philippines. The roads are dust or mud, depending on the weather.

"We met out in an open field where they had just completed a new bandstand. This was to be the site of the town plaza – some mañana. Prior to the meetings the sound truck went through the city, blaring the news that an American tenor would be giving a concert in the plaza. The people love singing, and they came by the hundreds.

"One little light bulb hung over my head as I sang. This one hundred-watt illumination dwindled to fifty watts by the time the other lights in the town went on, and every insect for miles around decided that it was convention time in the plaza. Around and around the bulb they flew – crawling in my hair, in my eyes, up my nose, on my ears, and down my shirt. There had been a time when I was so fearful of insects that with one fly in the air while I sang I would inhale each quick breath with dread. Now, during every song, they would fly in and out of my mouth – some to be inhaled, never to be seen again, and others to be spat out with my consonants. It was quite a choice. I never knew whether to swallow or spit.

"As I sat on the platform, discouraged with all of this, I thought, 'What if some fanatic out there would take a shot at us through the darkness? They would just dig a hole and say, "There lies another missionary." There isn't much notoriety in this. What am I doing out here anyway?'

"Then by His Holy Spirit, God began to move on the hearts of the people as Greg preached and I sang. Attitudes changed. Decisions were made. During the week more than three hundred in that little town acknowledged their need of Christ. By the end of the week, sixty were ready for baptism. On the final Sunday morning they stood with radiant faces, giving witness before the people of the town to their faith in Jesus Christ as Lord and Savior.

"As I sat in that two-hour-long baptismal service, God seemed to thunder the words to my heart and mind, 'THIS IS BIG BUSINESS!' There is nothing more important than the transformation of a life. People are more important than position, popularity, or wealth. What kind of a job – if it paid $1,000 a week – or a performance could possibly compare with this?

"Now when I face a businessman and he says, 'And, by the way, what's your line?' I respond, 'I am a missionary. And that is the biggest business in the world!' And if he is not convinced when I am through with him, at least he is convinced that I am convinced!'"

# ARE YOU DON OR DICK?

In 1955, I heard Don Hillis speak in Sacramento, California. I asked him if he would come for a week to our home in Marysville. In a few weeks Dick showed up and he insisted I call him Dick, not twin brother Don. This started a complete change in my life and lifestyle that continues today. His lifestyle became my goal for life.

> Vic Whetzel
> Former OC board member

# The "Dear John" Letter

From *Not Made for Quitting*, Dr. Dick Hillis (Minneapolis, MN: Dimension
Books, 1973), chapter 14, "The 'Dear John' Letter"

### Edward F. Murphy
*Missionary to South America under*
*Overseas Crusades, Inc.*
*Overseas Crusades Associate Executive*
*Director for Ministries*

My daughter Margaret Anne graduated from Culter
Academy in Los Angeles that weekend. At the baccalaureate
service I had eyes only for my sweet-sixteen.

The speaker was an angular man with a large forehead, gaunt
cheeks, and a lopsided chin – not handsome but magnetic. Probably
not yet thirty years old. His words soon captured my thoughts.

He spoke with power, with the authority of a man who knew the
Scriptures, with the controlled energy of one whose experience of
God was deep. As I listened to Ed Murphy that hot Sunday afternoon
the conviction formed in my mind: *Murphy belongs in South America.*

I flipped over my program and reread the blurb on the Reverend
Edward F. Murphy. Raised in the Catholic church, Biola graduate.
Now a pastor in a Los Angeles suburb.

I resolved to speak to him after the service. The graduation throng and my daughter, so grownup in her crisp new suit, detained me in the church. But I caught Murphy outside crossing the street to this car.

"Man," I told him as we shook hands, "that was a great message, but I wish you had preached it in South America. I believe God wants you on the foreign mission field."

"Dr. Hillis," Ed replied, "I've just been praying for months that God would show me exactly where He wants me. I am ready to go as soon as I know where and with what mission."

We made an appointment to talk about it that week. In my office Ed told me the amazing story of his missionary calling.

The name "Murphy" says Irish Catholic. Ed Murphy grew up in the Roman Catholic Church and was a devout, clean-living, loyal son of the church.

"Was it your conversion that made you leave Roman Catholicism?" I asked.

"No. Oddly enough, Dr. Hillis, my discovery that God wanted me to be a missionary forced me to break with my church. One of my friends raised the question, 'How are you going to be a missionary since you are a Roman Catholic? Will you enter the priesthood?'

"My answer startled *me*. 'No,' I replied instantly, 'I'm going to leave the Catholic church.'

"You see, Dr. Hillis, I realized that as a missionary I would have to preach salvation through Jesus Christ, not salvation through a church or its sacraments. Shall I tell you how I myself found salvation?"

I nodded and Mr. Murphy began his story.

In a summer forestry camp where he was working to save money for college, seventeen-year-old Ed looked for a friend whose conversation and conduct were clean. Soon he and Warren "Hutch" Hutchinson teamed up.

"Ed, are you a Christian?" Hutch asked as the two young men cleared a fire trail together one day.

"Why, sure! I'm a Roman Catholic," replied Ed in surprise.

"I know that," said his friend, "but are you a Christian?"

Hutch went on to explain that a Christian has experienced personally the salvation Jesus came to provide.

Murphy cut him short. How could a Protestant, separated from the true church, understand the things of God?

But deeply religious Murphy saw no reason why he should not have simple worship services with Protestant Hutch out among the California redwoods. Since there were no Sunday masses to attend, what harm could come from reading the Bible and praying together?

At first Murphy carried his missal to these quiet meetings. But more and more the words of the Scripture captivated him.

How simple and clear became the divine way of salvation as Ed heard and then read for himself the words of Jesus. The high school boy began to memorize: "I say emphatically that anyone who listens to My message and believes in God who sent me has eternal life, and will never be damned for his sins, but has already passed out of death into life" (John 5:24, *Living Gospels*).

Ed returned home in September a new creature in Christ but still an active Roman Catholic. His love for the New Testament which Hutch had given him was soon noticed by his family. They were upset by Ed's new religious concepts and arranged for him to attend indoctrination classes at the parish manse.

Yet the teaching of the priest could not take the place of the Word of God. Murphy read avidly. When forbidden to study the Scriptures at home he carried his New Testament to mass – it looked just like a missal – and read happily all through the service.

Graduating from high school Ed followed his electrical interests and began training at a trade school in Chicago. He rented a tiny apartment and threw all his spare time into the study of the new Douay Bible he bought.

Murphy had always supposed that the average layman would have great difficulty reading the Bible. But he discovered that the Holy Spirit illumined the pages for him.

"…Your own body does not belong to you, For God has bought you with a great price" (I Corinthians 6:19, 20, *Living Letters*) was the portion the divine light shone on one day.

For the first time Ed Murphy realized that by rights his life belonged to the Lord. The electrical career…was that God's plan for his life?

"O Lord," prayed the young student, "until now I did not know that I belonged only to you. Father, I am willing to do whatever you wish. Please show me you will."

Almost immediately, God showed him. Out of curiosity, Ed went to a Protestant church service with a friend. Neither the sermon nor the pastor impressed Murphy much. His friend left Ed waiting in the foyer for a few minutes after the service. A literature table stood nearby. Ed leafed through the magazines and pamphlets, picked up one, and took it home.

Carefully reading the booklet that night, Ed was stirred by the challenge of Christian missions. The pamphlet described the work of missionaries throughout the world. As Ed studied its message, the Holy Spirit engraved upon his heart the conviction that God wanted to use *him* in foreign service.

In the fall of 1948, Murphy knew he should leave school in Chicago and go home to California as his first step towards missionary service. But how was he to get the money for a two-thousand-mile trip? He could not ask his Catholic mother to loan him the money to quit electrical school, travel home, leave the Catholic church, and prepare himself for the mission field.

"A few days later," Ed states, "as I walked to school as usual, I was surprised to see a picket line around the school. Instructors and students were marching and carrying placards. The instructors had gone on strike for better working conditions.

"The school was closed down for some time. Every day I went to school hoping to attend classes, but I was always turned away by the pickets. 'Lord, what should I do now?' I prayed."

Obviously, by closing the door of the school God was opening Ed's door home. Now he could legitimately write and ask his mother to help him return to California. Soon Murphy was home again working to repay his mother's loan.

"Mom, God has called me to be a missionary," said Ed, coming right to the point as soon as he arrived home. "He has called me to preach the Gospel of His love and grace as taught in the Bible. I cannot reconcile this Gospel with many of the doctrines of our church, so I am leaving it. I want to prepare myself for the Lord's service."

Mrs. Murphy gaped at her son in amazement. She, of course, had known of Ed's love for the Bible and his "strange Protestant ideas." But she had never expected it to come to this.

"You are a Roman Catholic," she said, "and you will remain a Roman Catholic until you die. You are not going to leave your church. You are still my son and must do what I tell you."

Ed quietly replied that he must first obey God.

Through an aunt in Los Angeles he learned of Biola College. He was accepted as a student for the semester beginning in January. When Ed informed his mother, she was first furious, then heartbroken. In a few days she arranged an appointment for her son with the priest.

"My son," said the Reverend Father, when he and Ed were alone, "your life will end in ruin and the hand of God will be against you if you leave the church. The Roman Church is the only true church of Jesus Christ."

Murphy was only nineteen years old. All his knowledge of the Bible had come from his own private study during the past three years. How could he answer a learned priest? From the Catholic Bible, Ed showed the priest the basis for his faith in Christ and his decision to be a non-Catholic missionary.

"Father, no Protestant has led me astray. I am making my own decision on the basis of the Word of God."

"My son," returned the priest, "do you think you know the Scriptures better than we priests do? You are just a boy. You have not the training to enable you to interpret the Bible correctly. Only the Catholic church can expound its true teachings. You have read too much without guidance." And he offered Ed some books on Catholic doctrine.

Then the priest warned Ed of the conscqucnces of a break with the church. Ed would disgrace his family with its Irish Catholic tradition. He would be deserting his widowed mother in her hour of need. And he would bring down the judgments of God upon his head by forsaking the only storehouse of God's grace through which a man's soul could be saved.

Finally, seeing that Murphy turned to the Scriptures to counter each argument, the priest said, "The Bible commands children to obey their parents. Your mother has forbidden you to leave the Catholic church. If you disobey her, you will be disobeying the Bible which you claim is your guide for life."

What could the young Christian say to that? "Well, Father, I never thought of it that way before. The Bible certainly says, 'Children, obey your parents' (Ephesians 6:1). Therefore until my mother consents or until I am twenty-one, I suppose I cannot leave the Catholic church or begin my missionary training."

The priest went home in triumph and Mrs. Murphy heard the news with great delight. But Ed was in turmoil. For weeks his heart was torn in two directions.

"At last, Dr. Hillis, a ray of light seemed to shine on Jesus' words: 'I have come to set a man against his father, and …mother… But if you love your father and mother more than you love Me, you are not worthy of being Mine" (Matthew 10:35, 37, *Living Gospels*).

"I saw that my mother had placed herself in the way of God in my life. I realized that I must obey God even if in doing so I had to disobey my mother.

"'Mom,' I told her, 'I clearly see the will of God for my life. He has called me to preach the Gospel of His grace which comes to men through Jesus Christ, not through any one church, its priesthood or sacraments. I know you do not understand, but I must obey Christ and His Word.'

"For several hours we talked. Mother argued and pleaded. What agony for us both! Finally, weeping hysterically, Mother ran from the room crying, 'If you leave the church you are no son of mine.'

"Heartbroken, I packed my bags. I left my church, my home, and my embittered mother, and entered Biola College."

"Studies were hard at Biola," Murphy resumed his story. "I entered school at mid-year, and I hadn't the evangelical background of my fellow students. Often the phraseology and terminology used by the professors completely lost me. However, teachers and students helped me kindly. For a hungry new Christian, it was a thrilling experience.

"Then one morning I awoke to the thought, *What if the Roman Catholic Church is the only church of Jesus Christ after all? If the Roman church is true, then Ed Murphy is doomed to hell.*

"I was conscious of an evil presence in the room with me. Perhaps this sounds melodramatic to you, Dr. Hillis, but I felt that the Devil was standing there to claim me. What terrible oppression! I could not get out of bed. I was physically sick, mentally and emotionally tormented.

"I didn't go to classes that morning. I spent the whole day in bed, saying I was ill. How could I explain what was going on inside me?

"I knew that Jesus said, 'But some will come to Me – those the Father has given Me – and I will never, never reject them" (John 6:37, *Living Gospels*). I knew Jesus said, 'I give them eternal life, and they shall never perish. No one shall snatch them away from Me' (John 10:28, *Living Gospels*).

"Yet my heart was filled with terror and torment. I could not escape that accusing question, *What if the Roman church is right? Then you are doomed to hell.*

"Eventually I told my roommate what was happening to me. Soon many of the students were praying for me. Still I could not leave my bed or free myself of the awful fear that seemed to possess me.

"The third day was an all-school day of prayer, culminating in a united prayer meeting after supper. With my roommate's help, I got up and went to the auditorium. I sat down and tried to pray in my heart with the other students. At last, though I had never before prayed in public, I stood to my feet and cried out to God to deliver me from this terrible oppression. Immediately the evil presence with its fearsome accusations left me, and the joy of the Lord flooded my soul.

"Never again," continued Murphy, relief and gratitude shining in his grey eyes, "have I suffered such a demonic attack or been tempted to doubt the saving grace of God. 'No weapon that is formed against thee shall prosper,' says Isaiah 54:17 (KJV). But all this time another weapon was being formed against me, and this last one came closer than any of the others to breaking my will to serve God."

"You survived your mother's grief, the priest's arguments, and demonic oppression," I interposed. "I am surprised anything else could shake you, Ed."

"My fiancée wrote saying she would break our engagement if I persisted in my plans to become a missionary." Murphy's large eyes clouded at the memory.

"I told you, Dr. Hillis, that I had a pretty sweetheart. We had fallen in love when she was just a freshman in high school. We planned to marry in the summer after my first term at Biola. Lovely Loretta, sweet and sensitive! I dreamed of serving the Lord with her at my side. I knew she would follow me anywhere. When we first went together, she had agreed to join the Catholic church to marry me. And now that she was a born-again Christian I looked forward blissfully to our marriage and missionary work together."

"Then all of a sudden a 'Dear John' letter. Why?"

"Mother felt that the surest way to force me to abandon my plans for the Christian ministry would be through my love for Loretta. Loretta was young, impressionable, new in the faith. If she could be persuaded that she was not suited to mission work, perhaps she could talk me out of my commitment."

As a counselor of missionary candidates, I could well imagine the tack Mrs. Murphy had taken with Loretta.

"Loretta, do you really think that you have been made for that type of life? A delicate girl like you? Do you realize that missionaries live in grass huts in the jungle? You would have to carry water from a muddy river and boil it before you could drink it. Are you physically strong enough to keep house under such conditions?

"We really don't believe you have thought what such a move would involve. There's no sanitation and little medical care in those far-away lands. Your children would be born without a doctor's help. Sickness and dirt and evil climate would threaten their innocent lives. You'd better work on Ed now to get him to change his mind if you want a happy life and a healthy family.

"Tell Ed you are not the girl for missionary life. He'll change his plans for your sake. He might even come home from Bible school and go back to his electrical work. Then you could get married right away. He has three years of study ahead unless you can get him to see how unreasonable his missionary dream is."

Poor Loretta. A few months of that kind of pressure and no wonder she wrote Ed to cancel his plans, either for the mission field or for marriage.

"What did you do, Ed?" I asked.

"I left Biola right away, without even asking permission from the dean of men. I could have been expelled for that, Dr. Hillis, but I did not care. All that mattered was my poor scared sweetheart.

"I stayed home a week, trying to comfort and encourage her. But Loretta refused to consider being a missionary's wife. Eventually it came to a showdown. Loretta said I must choose between marrying her and being a missionary. I was heartbroken. I begged the Lord to change her mind. He seemed to say to me just what she had said, 'Which do you love best, Loretta or my will for you?'

"Dr. Hillis, I actually made plans to quit Biola. But God gave me strength to obey Him and faith to trust my life to His care.

"I went back to school, no longer engaged to the girl I deeply loved. I confess I had to continually fight the temptation to give up and go back to her.

"Before the school year was out, Loretta wrote that God had spoken to her. She confessed that she loved me and would serve God with me anywhere in the world.

"My mother was terribly upset. All her efforts had failed. Without telling me, she began to search the Scriptures and pray that God would help her to find His truth. When I arrived home for vacation after my second year at Biola, Mother greeted me with a radiant face.

"'Ed,' she said, hugging me, 'Jesus Christ is my personal Savior and Lord. I have placed all my confidence in His saving death and resurrection.'"

Ed paused, a wide smile wreathing his face as he remembered that happy meeting.

"Great, man. Marvelous," I exclaimed, as soon as I could trust my voice. "Everybody reconciled at last…you, your mother, Loretta. That is just the way God does things.

"But, Ed, you have been out of school six years. Why aren't you on the mission field?"

"I guess maybe I've been waiting to meet you, Dr. Hillis," said Murphy, grinning disarmingly. "Loretta and I applied to go to India right after graduation, but the Indian government turned down our visas. So we took a pastorate here in California.

"But lately I have been getting restless. I've corresponded with several missions. Right now I have application forms on my office desk all ready to mail. I have been asking the Lord, 'Where shall I go and with what mission?' And I've had a growing conviction that somehow, when the right time arrived, God would let me know.

"As I spoke to the Culter graduating class last Sunday, I spotted you in the audience, Dr. Hillis. I recognized you from hearing you in missionary conferences and from the Overseas Crusades literature I have been reading for years. Right away I thought, *Perhaps God will use Dr. Hillis to show me where and with what mission I should serve.*

"When you hailed me outside the church and said, 'Ed, God wants you to serve on the mission field,' my heart said, *This is it.* So here I am, boss. Do you have a job for me?"

"God has a job for you," I replied, "in South America."

# EPILOGUE

## Finishing Well in China
### (by OC missionary Keith Brown)

All during the dark, frightful years of the Cultural Revolution, I remember Dick Hillis constantly reminding his missionaries, "Don't stop praying for China. The doors will open again someday." When by God's grace they did open, it could clearly be seen that what Satan had meant for evil, God had meant for good that many might be saved for all eternity (see Genesis 50:20).

For it is not generally known that when Mao Tse-tung took over, he banned not only all Protestant and Catholic worship, but also Buddhist, Islamic, and all other religious observance. So people in China, particularly those under age 50, have no church, no religion, nothing. Anything that was religion was stopped. They grew up totally secular, atheist, and/or communist.

An unwitting result of this draconian measure was the creation of a great spiritual vacuum. God has created us as spiritual beings. It goes back to the fact God has built Himself in all of us, and even fifty years and the Cultural Revolution can in no way stamp out this inner desire. People are going to worship something. Despite government oppression, the hunger for the spiritual is still there.

In China, this hunger can be found particularly among students. In my visits inside the mainland, students have told us over and over that communism has been an abject failure. Right now it is the only government they have, but they realize there is something more. "We are really searching," they tell me.

That the very ripe population of China is being evangelized is almost self-evident. From a virtual flat beginning in the 1950s, the "official" number of Christians is now counted at 40 million, but most observers think there are at least 100 million. There could be 200 million, or even more. It is impossible to count, especially when you take in the vast populations in remote areas. There could even be tens of millions of secret believers that are not accounted for.

That these statistics do not simply represent hands raised at an evangelistic crusade—impossible in China anyway—is reflected in the number of congregations on the mainland. Again, nobody knows how many exist. I believe there are about 17,000 Three Self Patriotic Movement (TSPM) churches "approved" by the Peking government. In addition, it is not realized by many that there is also a bigger number of registered house churches that the government also recognizes.

Beyond the approved lists are many tens of thousands of other house churches, some say as many as 100,000 total churches or meeting places where believers gather regularly.

The major contributor to the massive evangelism taking place seems to be through the ministry of radio. I take this from James Taylor III, grandson of pioneer China missionary J. Hudson Taylor. Now in his seventies and still living in Hong Kong, he probably knows more about China than any other living American. It is his observation that about 50 percent of all believers in China today have come to the Lord because of Christian radio. Since 70 percent of listeners now are college and high school students, this paints a bright picture for the future.

Just as radio has played a crucial role in evangelizing the millions on China's mainland, so now is radio playing a crucial role in the discipling and training of believers and their pastors. Dick Hillis could visualize this when he first heard of the Village Friendship Seminary (now Voice of Friendship Seminary) radio program of the Far East Broadcasting Company. He could easily picture a host of inexperienced pastors and their congregations needing further training in every aspect of church life and ministry. In 1982 he therefore joined forces with FEBC. If they would produce and broadcast the program, Dick would see that the money was provided for it.

In my role as the fundraiser for the Voice of Friendship Seminary and coordinator between OC and the Far East Broadcasting Company, I see hundreds of letters that tell of just this need and the opportunity it presents. Over and over listeners write to say, "We come for fellowship in church, but we tend to hear the same thing over and over. Our pastor is not educated and few of the rest of us read or write." Training these pastors represents the big need for the church in China.

For example, the unregistered house church pastors cannot go to one of the seventeen or eighteen government-approved seminaries such as the largest one in Nanching with its 300 to 400 students. Even if they could, house church pastors would not have the educational qualifications nor the money to get into seminary.

So there are literally thousands of men and women pastoring churches with no background in Christianity or even in religion at all. Many have only a Bible, but no concordance, much less a commentary. Suddenly they are in pastoral leadership. Where do they go for help?

To radio, as did this listener:

> One day I turned to your station and was deeply touched by the messages in the programs. I listened a few nights and decided to become a Christian and repented before the Lord. After a while, I got involved in the ministry of the local church. I listened to the radio, wrote down the notes and delivered sermons for the church. I am now a full-time minister.

This process is constantly repeated. Many are converted through listening to a radio broadcast. A good portion of these converts begin attending a local church. Some of them get biblical training through Christian radio and even begin preaching. A few become full-time pastors.

The daily broadcast is designed to be like a little seminary over the radio. If listeners are faithful in studying the workbooks for two years, they probably get the equivalent of at least one year of Bible college study. The results can be seen in letters from the thousands that flow into the FEBC offices in Hong Kong:

> In just a decade we have developed and taken care of 21 churches. Our workers have been tuning in to your station. I advise them to listen to your programs more often to enhance their biblical knowledge, but also to take good care of their church. Frankly speaking, I have not received any formal training in theology. In my service and ministry over the past decade I have accumulated sermon notes of one meter high, a product of the seeds you have sown from the broadcasts I have listened to.

When OC first started helping to fund the Voice of Friendship Seminary program, about one letter a month would come in. In 2004, FEBC received 31,477 responses from their total programming to China, including 6,760 sent to the Voice of Friendship Seminary program. But for every letter received, there undoubtedly are thousands of pastors being trained who never write, who don't know how to write, or who do not even have easy access to buying a stamp!

With transmitter sites in Korea, Saipan, the Philippines, and Guam, FEBC radio literally covers all of China except for the far western extreme cut off by mountain ranges. The Voice of Friendship Seminary program always receives by a very large margin the most responses of any FEBC programs beamed to the mainland.

When the radio ministry first began broadcasting, Hillis said to me, "This is so great. I began my ministry in China fifty years ago, and now that I'm toward the end of my life I'm able to finish my ministry back in China."

Along with his passion for the lost and for training pastors, Dick's life message was a constant encouragement for believers to lay up treasures in heaven. Having read this book from the heart of Dick Hillis, and especially this chapter of his continuing ministry to China through radio, you might ask the Lord how He would have you participate in a legacy fund for an indefinite continuation of the Voice of Friendship Seminary program.

For further information, write or call OC. Checks should be made out to "OC International" and noted separately for "China Radio." Donations may also be made online at **ONECHALLENGE.org**.

# LET CHRIST BE LORD

Let Christ be Lord
And I His servant
Let Christ be God, Master and King
Let my desire
Be for His glory
My lips His praise
Forever sing

Let Christ be Lord
And I His servant
His Spirit fill my every part
To be conformed
Into His image
My will, His will
My heart, His heart

Let Christ be Lord
Feared and adored
Praised and implored
Let Christ be Lord

Let Christ be Lord
And I his servant
Just to obey His Word and go
Into this world
So lost and dying
Pour out my life
That His may show

Jeff Boesel
Director, Mobilization
OC International